Suicide: Ireland's Story

EMILY COX

BLACKWATER PRESS

Editor
Frieda Donohue

Design & Layout
Paula Byrne

Cover Design
Karen Hoey

ISBN
1-84131-804-3

Produced in Ireland by
Blackwater Press
c/o Folens Publishers
Hibernian Industrial Estate
Tallaght
Dublin 24

Acknowledgements

I would like to thank all of the individuals and families who let me into their lives and who shared their personal stories openly and honestly in the hope of raising awareness of the issue of suicide in Ireland and reaching out to others in need.

Thanks to Anne Walsh and family; Mary and John McTernan, Cáit Kerins, Carmel Fallon and STOP; Maureen Bolger, Eithne Dunne and Teen-Line; Jean Casey, Pat Buckley and the Let's Get Together Foundation; Philip McTaggart and PIPS; Nuala Whelan and family; Tim; Mary O'Connell; Paul from Console; Billie from the Red Ribbon Project and Elaine Doyle.

Thanks to all of the individuals and organisations for their time and assistance with my research. Thanks to Josephine Scott and the Irish Association of Suicidology; Paul Corcoran and the National Suicide Research Foundation; Reverend Dr Tony Byrne; Sr Kathleen Maguire; Schizophrenia Ireland and John Saunders; Aware and Sandra Hogan; Paul and the staff at Console; Ronan Maguire BL; Elaine Keogh; Michael Egan and Living Links; Fr Aidan Troy; Sr Sheila O'Kelly of Wicklow Living Links; the Bishop of Cork, the Right Reverend Paul Colton and Janet Maxwell and the Representative body of the Church of Ireland; Roisin Meenan; Fr Pat O'Donoghue; Dr Patricia Casey; the Irish Catholic Bishops; Governor John Lonergan, Fiona Moran and the staff at Mountjoy Prison; Paul Madden of the Southern Gay Men's Health Project; Bruno Nicolai of the Sexual Health Centre; Ciaran McKinney from Gay HIV Strategies; Bernadine Quinn of Dundalk Outcomers; Michael Barron of BeLonG To; Louise Tierney; Petra Jäppinen and the staff of Outhouse; Catherine Power of sOUTh; Ronnie Fay from Pavee Point; Paddy Wilson and volunteers at Foyle Search and Rescue; David Linehan; Prof. Ivan J. Perry and the National

Parasuicide Registry; Niamh Nic Daéid; Kathleen O'Connor, Director of Pastoral Care, Adelaide and Meath Hospital; Paddy Shannon of Childline NI; and the Abbey Manor Hotel in Dromahair, Co. Leitrim.

Thanks to the staff of UCD and Trinity libraries; *The Irish Times*; Amanda Dunleavy and *The Late Late Show*; the National Education Psychological Service; the American Association of Suicidology; the Samaritans; the authors of the *Report of the National Task Force on Suicide* (1998); the authors of *Reach Out*; and the Department of Health and Children.

Thanks to all my friends and colleagues for their help and support – particularly Keith, Anne, Doireann and Nuala. Special thanks to Bronagh for working with me into the early hours on many occasions.

Thanks to my family – Des, Imelda, Brian Sr, Valerie, Brian Jr, Eoin, Maeve and Aengus – for their help and support. Special thanks to Aengus, Maeve and Dad for chauffeuring me around the country and to Maeve for the additional help and proof-reading. Thanks to my mum, Valerie, for the vital support, advice and encouragement she gave me.

I would particularly like to thank Dr John F. Connolly, Secretary of the Irish Association of Suicidology, for his availability, advice and suggestions and for taking the time to read my manuscript in full.

Finally, thanks to my editor, Frieda Donohue, for her dedication and commitment and who, despite numerous challenges from the author, succeeded in keeping her patience throughout.

Contents

Introduction

This book came about as a result of meeting John and Mary McTernan from Dromahair in Co. Leitrim. In January 2004, they were devastated when their only son, 24-year-old Garry, died by suicide. Garry's parents were completely shocked – everything had seemed fine; there had been no obvious indication that he was planning to take his life. For the McTernans, a parents' worst nightmare had become a reality and they knew their lives would never be the same again.

Losing a child, especially one so young, is extremely traumatic for the child's mother and father. Parents do not expect to bury their children – when that child dies by his or her own hand, the trauma is only intensified. The family tortures itself, desperately speculating why their child did not come to them for help and wondering if they could have prevented the suicide.

Shortly after Garry's death, the McTernans came into contact with two other local families who had lost loved ones to suicide. Cáit Kerins had lost her 27-year-old brother, Pat, to suicide in November 2000 and four months after Garry's death, Carmel Fallon lost her 25-year-old son, Kevin, to suicide. The families, all from the same small village of Dromahair, came together and decided that they had to do something to prevent the tragedy of suicide, so that other families would be spared the agony in the future.

In 2004, the three families set up STOP (Suicide, Teach, Organise, Prevent), with a view to raising awareness of suicide in Ireland. Following the nightmare each of these families had been through, they resolved to reach out and help other families who had been bereaved by suicide, offering support and assistance to distraught people in desperate need of help. In February 2005, they asked me to help publicise the STOP conference they were organising in Dromahair. The aim of the conference was to raise awareness of suicide in Ireland as a step towards developing an understanding of the problem and with a view to future prevention.

Through my work with STOP, I met a lot of families who had lost loved ones to suicide, as well as professionals who worked in the field. I realised what a serious problem suicide had become in modern Ireland. I also discovered that, although a vast amount of research and prevention work has been carried out to date, the general public still does not know a great deal about suicide in Ireland. Indeed, people are continually shocked at the fact that suicide is a greater killer than road accidents in this country. Suicide is not a popular topic of conversation – people hope that it won't touch their lives and there is a fear that talking about suicide could put the idea in people's minds. The fact is, however, that the only way to understand what causes suicide and to move towards preventing it is to talk about it openly and honestly.

I haven't written this book with a specific reader in mind: it is aimed at everyone and its goal is to raise awareness of the issues surrounding suicide. I also hope, in some small way, to reach out to people who have been bereaved by suicide Through the stories of others, I hope to help them to realise that although life will never be the same again, it does go on and there is help available out there.

There is no fixed order in which you should read this book. Some of you might prefer to read the personal stories first. Others might prefer the more technical sections, where you can gain a general overview of suicide in Ireland.

OVERVIEW OF SUICIDE IN IRELAND

In Ireland in 2004, 457 people took their own lives, making suicide a greater cause of death than road accidents. While there is significant investment into the prevention of road deaths and rightly so, experts say that the area of mental health has been seriously neglected.

Suicide has risen considerably in Ireland with a seven-fold increase in the number of deaths by suicide in the Republic between the early 1960s and the first decade of the twenty-first century. Considering that every suicide has a serious impact on at least six people, there are very few residents in Ireland who have not, in some way, been touched by the knock-on effects of such a tragic death.

While there has been a tremendous increase in suicide in Ireland, it is not a problem specific to Ireland as the rate has risen worldwide in recent decades. Approximately one million people die by suicide worldwide each year. In a recent study of 25 OECD countries, Ireland had the seventeenth highest rate of suicide. However, the rate of youth suicide is particularly high in Ireland and we have the fifth highest in the European Union (World Health Organisation, 2005). Overall, men account for a massive 80 per cent of all suicides in Ireland, and the rate is particularly high among young men (those in the 15–24 and 24–35 age groups), with suicide being the number one cause of death in males aged between 15 and 24.

And these figures don't reflect the huge number of attempted suicides – Accident and Emergency is confronted with 10,000 attempted suicides in Ireland every year. Secretary of the Irish Association of Suicidology (IAS), Dr John Connolly, estimates that this could be as low as a fifth of the real level of attempted suicides, as most people who harm themselves do not go to casualty departments. A previous suicide attempt is a serious warning sign and considered a strong predictor of future attempts and of completed suicide. One in three Irish people who die by suicide have made a previous attempt to take their own life.

WHY?

What is it about modern Irish society that drives so many individuals to such extreme measures? Why are people, and particularly young men, so desperate that they see no other way out than to end it all? There are no clear-cut answers.

Mental illness and the effects it can have on an individual's personal relationships and work and social life can result in feelings of hopelessness. Mental illness is considered to be a factor in up to 90 per cent of all suicides, and mental illnesses, such as depression, and especially severe mental illnesses, such as schizophrenia and bipolar disorder, are considered a major risk factor for suicide.

International research has found that more than half of all suicides are associated with depression. Often, as will be seen in many of the personal stories in this book, people close to the individual who died by suicide noticed no signs of depression; however, with the benefit of hindsight, families often realise retrospectively that their loved one may have been depressed. It is vital to understand, however, that, of the people who suffer from depression or other mental illness, only a very small minority take their lives.

The attitude of the Church and the fact that suicide was a crime meant that, in the past, suicides often went unreported in Ireland. Indeed, suicide was only decriminalised in Ireland in 1993. In the past, the Catholic Church viewed suicide as a mortal sin, refusing to allow a person who died by suicide to be buried in consecrated grounds. The Catholic Church is much more sympathetic nowadays.

There was a considerable increase in suicide in Ireland in the 1980s and 1990s, a time that saw vast changes in Ireland's economic situation. Unsurprisingly, perhaps, amid the economic depression, high unemployment and associated poverty of the 1980s and early 1990s, Ireland's suicide rate saw an increase. Less predictably, however, the economic boom that transformed the country in the late 1990s was accompanied by an unprecedented rise in the rate of suicide, particularly among the young. So, while the Celtic Tiger was responsible for huge economic success, in 1998 Ireland recorded its highest-ever rate of suicide.

With the advent of the Celtic Tiger and the diminished role of Church and family, Ireland has undergone significant social change in the last decade. Research has shown that countries which undergo major social change can experience a rise in suicide rates, especially among young people. This appears to be a trend in modern Ireland.

Aware, a voluntary organisation that supports those affected by depression, points to studies that show an increase in the rate of mild to moderate depression since 1945. They point out that this suggests that social change may be relevant to the increased rate of environmentally determined mood disorders.

At the STOP Conference in February of 2005, Rev. Dr Tony Byrne pointed out that 1998 was the year of the Celtic Tiger, and a time of sudden economic growth. 'People were disenchanted with having more, but not being more.' In his book *Suicide Awareness*, Dan Neville TD, President of the IAS, refers to a New Zealand Report on young suicides which states 'the prevailing materialistic, worldly values that equate individual success with wealth, good looks and power make young people feel quite worthless and cast out by society'.

The IAS recognises that there are increased social pressures in Ireland today, especially on young people. There are huge expectations of young people to succeed in all areas of life. Image pressures, accentuated by media portrayals of perfection, academic pressures, sexual pressures and career pressures are all heaped on young people. If young people don't achieve the high standards expected of them in this fast-moving society, they may feel they have failed and feelings of failure and rejection are associated with suicidal behaviour.

Economic growth is not, in itself, a negative thing and the quality of life in Ireland has improved dramatically as a result of the Celtic Tiger. The manner in which society progresses can, however, take its toll emotionally, and though, once again, it is not possible to point at the exact reasons why, certain trends in society appear to rise in tandem with the suicide rates; this may indicate that similar forces play a role in each.

Religion no longer plays the pivotal role it once did in Irish society; the marriage rate has dropped, there has been a significant increase in separation and divorce and the number of children born outside wedlock has increased dramatically. Hospitals are admitting more and more patients for alcoholism. Crime rates have risen considerably. The sense of security once offered by stable family structures and the unchanging power of the Church is no longer available; both of these forces have broken down and people can feel like they don't have any beliefs to hold firm to when things are difficult. They can feel like they have been cast adrift without anything to hold on to.

While the rate of male suicide has always been much higher than female, males can be particularly vulnerable to the changes brought about by modern times. The ratio of deaths by suicide for men and women in Ireland is four to one. One key element of society's progression is gender equality.

Back in 1960s Ireland, it was widely accepted that a woman's place was in the home; in the mid-twentieth century, it was still considered normal for women to give up their civil service jobs upon marriage. Now, women compete with men academically and in the workplace and while this progress is clearly right and positive, it has resulted in some confusion and poor self-image among men. They have found it difficult to identify a new role for themselves in this changed society and have struggled to maintain a sense of self. Rev. Dr Tony Byrne comments, 'Men used to have a macho image; now, with the gender balance transition, they are trying to find a new role.' He also points out that, although not necessarily intended maliciously, there is propaganda against men. 'You would think every man is a dumbo.' Society is, in his opinion, also guilty of sending mixed messages to men: on the one hand, the macho role of the male is considered defunct; on the other hand, men are still made fun of for acting less than macho. He also feels that in modern times women are more independent and act as though they don't need men.

Dr John Connolly points to the fact that men tend to suppress their emotions and internalise their problems as a determining factor in higher suicide rates among men. 'Big boys don't cry.' The fact that men don't cry is societal. Men are less well-integrated into society. Women are more inclined to talk about their problems – they may 'bitch'. There is a protective factor with women; they network better. They are more talkative and much more likely to seek help. They are also typically more involved in religion and are less likely to have an alcohol problem. Furthermore, men tend to use more violent methods when attempting to take their lives, meaning that their chances of surviving the attempt are much lower. While the suicide rates among women did increase in the 1970s and 1980s, the overall rate for women has not increased in the past 15 years. This is due to a decrease in suicide among older women. However, there has been a marked increase in the rate of suicide among young women in recent years.

Suicide in Ireland appears to be more of a rural problem than an urban one, with rates per 100,000 in Dublin and more urbanised counties generally lower than the rest of the country. This is typical of most European countries and could be partially explained by easier access to health services in urban areas, as well as by the increased risk of isolation in rural areas.

FACTORS ASSOCIATED WITH SUICIDE

People who take their own lives come from every stratum of society – men and women, teenagers and the elderly, rich and poor. It is a problem in our society that nobody can fully explain or understand.

The loss felt following the death of a loved one can have a profound effect on some individuals. Death is a part of life and nearly everyone will experience the loss of someone close to them at some stage. Certainly, most people will not feel the need to resort to drastic measures because of it. However, each person and each situation is unique and bereavement does count among the factors affecting the suicide rate. The loss of a family member to suicide further increases the risk of suicide for other members of that family.

Loss and feelings of hopelessness following the breakdown of a relationship can also have a particularly devastating effect on some people, as can an argument with family or friends. These are environmental factors that are connected to suicide. Still, it is again noteworthy that relationships break up every minute of the day and people generally cope with the effects and get on with their lives. In an isolated context, if an individual does not suffer from a psychiatric illness and has no other major problems in his or her life, it would be most unlikely that that person would turn to something as drastic as suicide. Males tend to cope less well with the breakdown of relationships than females, which could play a role in the over-representation of men.

Unemployment can have a significant effect on an individual's psychological well-being, and studies show that the unemployed are six times more likely to be suffering from a psychiatric disorder (*Suicide Awareness*, Dan Neville TD). People are often defined by society in terms of their careers and, indeed, society tends to label people according to their position of employment. When a person is unemployed, it can diminish their own self-image and self-worth. Other situations associated with hopelessness include financial problems and hugely challenging life experiences, such as being imprisoned.

Alcohol and substance misuse are also cited as being risk factors for suicide. Dr John Connolly says that alcohol is associated with 45 per cent of all suicides. Once again, alcohol itself does not cause suicide, but it has been suggested that many of the problems that lead a person to contemplate taking his or her life can be similar to those factors that lead an individual to abuse alcohol. Considering the high levels of youth suicide in Ireland, it is noteworthy that young people in Ireland are also drinking more, and are more likely than their older counterparts to engage in binge drinking. (The subject of alcohol and suicide is explored in greater depth later in this book.)

Physical illness, especially debilitating or terminal illness, is considered a risk factor for suicide.

During times of war, suicide levels can go down – this was the case during both of the World Wars. In Northern Ireland, the suicide rate went down during the Troubles and increased following the ceasefire and the Good Friday Agreement. These figures could be partially explained by a heightened instinct for survival when under attack, as well as by the sense of belonging and solidarity that exists in a community that perceives itself as sharing a common threat. Still, the factors that lead to suicide are generally complex and it would be over-simplistic to explain the lower rate of suicide during wartime simply in these terms.

SUICIDE AND THE MEDIA

Suicide represented in theatre, in films or in soap operas may influence some people to use the method portrayed. The IAS refers to a popular English TV series, which, in 1996, dramatised a suicide attempt by overdose. 'Following that programme, there was an increase in the number of people admitted to casualty departments following suicide attempts by the same method. This and other studies suggest that descriptions of the method of suicide may have inherent dangers.' The IAS says other programmes, handled in the right way, could serve to educate the public and even play a part in preventing suicidal behaviour.

The portrayal of suicide in the media may also play a role in increasing the risk of suicide. For example, if presented in a glamorous or heroic manner, there could be a danger of copycat suicides, which are believed to account for 5 per cent of suicides in young people. The IAS, in partnership with the Samaritans, has developed a series of media guidelines for reporting suicide and they say that the media generally works in partnership with the IAS in adhering to these guidelines. This is not always the case, however, and the IAS points out that, 'Experts feel that the media can have a positive or negative effect on vulnerable groups. In particular, the young are especially susceptible.'

Support for this theory came following the tragic suicide of Nirvana's lead singer, Kurt Cobain, in Seattle in 1994. While experts feared a rise in copycat suicides among local fans, this was not the case. They believe that this was due to the media handling of Cobain's death – it was in no way glamorised and it emphasised the tragic loss of life. The media also published helpline numbers and, while calls to these lines increased after Cobain's death, the number of suicides did not. Suicide and the media is discussed in more depth later in this book. For full details on media guidelines, see the IAS website (www.ias.ie).

REDUCING THE STIGMA OF SUICIDE

Suicide was once a seriously taboo word and not just because it was deemed a crime by the state and a mortal sin by the Church. Society associated suicide with 'madness' – indeed, mental illness was also highly stigmatised and little understood. There was a perception that if a person died by suicide, there was something 'not quite right' in that person's family. Hence, it was once commonplace for people to cover up the fact that a loved one had died by suicide for fear of what other people would think and say. That shame often meant that friends and neighbours were at a complete loss to know what to say when confronted with suicide. As a result, bereaved families were often isolated in their grief – while deaths by causes other than suicide would draw a constant stream of neighbours and friends to sympathise and offer support, people would avoid those grieving the loss of a loved one through suicide.

As the personal stories in this book show, human contact and the opportunity to talk is the one thing that bereaved people need most. Devastated by the tragic loss of a loved one, the bereaved have to try to come to terms with the fact that the person chose to take their life and deal with the resulting emotional destruction – denial, confusion, anger, guilt and depression. People who have lost close family members or friends to suicide have an increased risk of taking their own lives and in some families there have been a series of suicides. Experts warn that, in particular, the person who finds the body of someone who has taken their own life needs to be watched for suicide risk.

Since the decriminalisation of suicide, Irish society has become much more understanding and informed about suicide. Our health services have made strides in the area of mental health and programmes promoting positive mental health have been introduced in Irish schools. Illnesses such as depression are no longer covered up and people are much more likely to recognise their illness and seek treatment. The work of organisations such as Aware has brought the issue of mental illness into the public arena.

There are a number of factors considered to protect against suicide. These include strong faith or religious belief, marriage, a sense of 'social-connectedness' (a strong involvement in life through work, family, friends, sports and hobbies), close emotional relationships, high self-esteem and problem-solving skills. Most of these factors give people a purpose and a sense of hope. Strong, close friendships and good family relationships make it easier for a person to discuss issues that may be bothering them. As communication and talking about problems are counted among the possible factors in the lower suicide rate among women, it is essential to have someone to talk to and essential for people to realise that it is not a weakness to discuss their problems.

TOWARDS PREVENTING SUICIDE

In the hope of raising awareness of the issue of suicide in Ireland, this book has not been written with one specific type of reader in mind: it is aimed at everyone. There are many ways in which suicide can be prevented, but any approach needs to be integrated across all areas of our lives: from health and education to politics, religion, the law, the media and society at large. Preventing suicide is everyone's responsibility and while medical experts play a crucial role in assessing suicide risk and diagnosing and treating mental health problems, suicide cannot be prevented by these means alone. Everyone should be part of the solution.

People who are suicidal don't really want to die; they just can't bear the pain they are in. They feel the sadness will never end and feel they are unable to take control. They can't make decisions and believe there is no way out of the agony. If you want to help someone you feel may be at risk from suicide, make sure you know the warning signs (see the back of this book), make yourself available to them, and listen to them. Don't ever say you understand how they feel because this will take away any sense of trust: they will feel you can't possibly know what they are going through. Do not be judgemental because when someone has reached this point of desperation, it is of no help to preach the value of life and the immorality of suicide. Nor is it advisable to act shocked if someone says they are contemplating suicide, as this will make them more reluctant to trust you with their problems. If you are concerned about someone, it is important to listen carefully to determine the level of risk. To find out how immediate the risk is, they should be asked how specific their plan is: do they have a specific date, time and means of taking their life in mind? If the person is high-risk, it is advisable to put them in touch with their GP and, if at all possible, remove any means that they can use to take their life (e.g. firearms, toxic substances etc.). Do not try to deal with the problem alone. Share the problem and get support.

As well as being prepared to recognise and assist in suicide prevention in the case of immediate risk, everyone can play a role in suicide prevention on a broader level, whether it is helping to promote awareness and reduce stigma, adhering to IAS guidelines when writing on the subject in the media or playing an active role in promoting positive mental health through the health and education systems. Since the establishment of the IAS in 1996, there has been much more open debate and attention has been drawn to the need for research. Huge investment, both in terms of time and money, has been made in studying the nature of suicide in Ireland and throughout the world. Still, it remains a complex problem that nobody can fully understand or explain. Continued investment in research is essential in order to identify the factors associated with suicide, and to learn more about the factors already identified. We need to understand why some individuals choose to end it all, while others appear to find coping strategies that allow them to deal with the problems that life presents in a positive fashion. The National Suicide Research Foundation, devoted to carrying out research in the area, continues to increase Ireland-specific research, which highlights the urgent areas which should be targeted. As it is recognised that mental illness is associated with the majority of suicides, this is an area that it is vital to target in order to prevent suicide.

As well as treating existing problems that can lead to helplessness and hopelessness and, in extreme cases, suicide, it is widely acknowledged that there should be a strong focus on promoting positive mental health generally and educating people on how to cope with life's difficulties.

One area that the IAS has focused particular attention on is reducing the levels of suicide in schools. A number of conferences have been held in Ireland over the last 10 years, attended by school principals and teachers, as well as mental health professionals and national and international experts in the area of suicide prevention. These conferences have been organised to facilitate the exchange of information about suicide, the development of a better understanding of the nature of suicide risk in schools, and the exploration of the role of schools in promoting positive mental health. Following on from these conferences and drawing on research from both Ireland and abroad, the IAS has introduced a number of suicide prevention guidelines into schools, including crisis intervention and emergency response programmes, as well as best practise guidelines.

All interested parties should continue to lobby public representatives to ensure that suicide prevention and the promotion of positive mental health remain high on their agendas.

The Irish Association of Suicidology maintains that suicide prevention is everybody's responsibility. By being aware of the signs and symptoms of suicide risk and the factors that prevent against suicide, a proactive approach to suicide prevention can be taken.

In September 2005, the Department of Health and Children, together with the Health Service Executive, launched 'Reach Out – National Strategy for Action on Suicide Prevention 2005–2014'. The government's 10-year suicide prevention strategy includes 20 areas to target for action. As well as laying out aims and objectives for targeting the various areas associated with suicide, the strategy provides for the immediate establishment of a National Office for Suicide Prevention within the Health Service Executive, new services for the treatment of self-harm in hospitals and A&E wards, the development of bereavement support services and a major national campaign to promote positive mental health. The 10-year strategy builds on the work of the 1998 National Task Force on Suicide.

THE PERSONAL STORIES IN THIS BOOK

This book tells a number of stories of families who have lost loved ones to suicide, either recently or a number of decades ago. These personal stories highlight the very real tragedy of suicide in this country and the important role everyone has in taking a sensitive approach to families who have suffered such a terrible loss. While, by the very nature of the subject of this book, these stories are extremely sad, I feel they are of the utmost importance in highlighting the nature of suicide and the extreme effects it will have on a family or community. The stories of the pain of those left behind after a suicide highlight what a serious problem suicide is and how vital it is to raise awareness of it. Sharing information may serve to decrease the occurrence of suicide in Ireland.

TERMINOLOGY

In this book, I do not use the term 'commit suicide' on the advice of professionals in the area, as this indicates that the deceased has committed a crime even though suicide is no longer a crime in Ireland. Instead, I use the terms 'lost by suicide', 'died by suicide' or 'took one's life'. It is important not to use the term 'commit suicide', which carries the old stigma of committing a sin and can cause further pain to a family already suffering tremendously after a loved one has taken their own life.

Garry McTernan

In less than five years, three families from the small village of Dromahair, Co. Leitrim lost their sons to suicide. Garry McTernan took his life two days after his 24th birthday in January 2004; Pat Kerins died by suicide at the age of 27 in November 2000 and Kevin Fallon took his life in May 2004, aged 24. Following the deaths of their loved ones, the three families have done extensive work in highlighting the problem of suicide through conferences and the media. They founded the organisation STOP (Suicide, Teach, Organise, Prevent).

Garry, Pat and Kevin are representative of the worrying level of suicide rates in Ireland, particularly amongst young men. Though the overall rate of suicide in Ireland is average compared to other European countries, men under 35 years account for approximately 40 per cent of all Irish suicides. Of the 444 people to die by suicide in Ireland in 2003, 175 were males under the age of 35. The first three chapters in this book tell the stories of these three boys from Dromahair whose lives ended tragically in suicide. As with all suicides, the family and friends of Garry, Kevin and Pat are left behind, devastated by the untimely, shocking deaths of their loved ones.

It is incredibly difficult for Garry's parents, John and Mary McTernan, to cope with Garry's death and they don't want other families to have to go through the same anguish.

Garry died on 9 January 2004. He had just turned 24. His suicide came completely out of the blue and the family was traumatised.

'There was no indication at the time, though we did learn a lot in hindsight.'

Garry worked in a factory in Manorhamilton. 'He was easy-going, calm and cool. He was a good-looking guy, big into his music. He had loads of CDs.' His mother Mary says he was a good, caring son with a lot of friends. Mary was very close to her son. 'He told me everything about his life, work, girls … we talked about it all.' Garry was also a Corporal in the FCA, which was very important to him and Mary said that he was thrilled about it. 'He was a friendly guy, pleasant and helpful and happy. He would go out with his friends, but was a bit of a home bird. He loved television.' Garry was also hugely involved with Young Fine Gael. He had no major problems in life and only drank occasionally. He did have some emotional 'stuff' with girlfriends, which he shared with his mother. 'Of all people, he was someone you'd never believe would self-harm. As a kid, he was into karate. He loved music and cars and kept his car cleaned and polished.'

On the day Garry died, he had been out in the back garden with his mother and their black labrador, Lucy. It didn't for a moment appear that he was thinking of not being around after that day. 'He had said to me he was thinking of going shopping for clothes at the weekend and asked would I come with him as he always did. I said I would.' Later on, Garry was working on the computer and then headed out. 'At about 9.30 he came home. I remember he was sitting on the chair and he was very tense. I went to bed early.' Garry stayed up with his dad, John, watching a film. Then John went to bed and left Garry watching television.

John got up at 7.30 the next morning. The television was still on but Garry wasn't there. John noticed Garry's mobile phone on the table, which he thought was a little strange. Then, he noticed a light on in the garage and went out to investigate. He found his son hanging inside. From that moment, the McTernans' lives would be turned upside down forever. Garry had left a suicide note, 'saying he loved us and we were to be happy'.

The family was filled with disbelief. 'His friends, like ourselves, were totally shocked. They could not believe this [had] happened to

Garry – they still can't.' Mary spoke to all of Garry's closest friends after his death, but they had no inkling as to why it had happened either. 'They, like ourselves, can't find any answers.'

'Hindsight' is a word that figures frequently in nearly all of the personal stories in this book – and it is a lot easier to pick out the signs looking back, though they generally are very subtle at the time. 'Looking back, we can see that he did have slight mood swings, but we all do. In hindsight, we can see he was depressed and he did talk about death.' Mary now believes that her son had just given up: 'I was too close to him to notice. What happened was a horrendous shock and every parent's worst nightmare. One day you have a very fine son you love to bits, the next day he's not around anymore.' Garry didn't have a girlfriend and he used to worry about this. 'He would ask me why girls he liked just wanted to be his friend and not go out with him. He didn't have any long-term relationship.'

The family also realised later that Garry had intentionally given away his ATM card three weeks before he died. 'He said, "Mum, look after this for me," and he also told us the three songs he wanted played at his funeral if he died in a car crash … he had been saying that for about two months.'

Mary also wondered why she, as a psychiatric nurse by profession, hadn't noticed anything herself. 'I have always said to myself that I should have seen something, but even our family GP, who knew Garry very well, didn't notice anything, either.' Mary now feels that she was too close to Garry to realise that there was something amiss.

Mary has done a huge amount of research into suicide since Garry's death and she understands that there had to have been something wrong with him for him to do something so drastic. 'I realise that Garry wasn't rational when he took his own life. That wasn't the way he was, as a character – he had to have been depressed. In a rational frame of mind he wouldn't do that.'

'I was never angry with him, none of the family was. How could you be angry with someone who was not rational when he decided to take his life?' She is certain that Garry wasn't in a logical enough state of mind to think of the devastating effect his death would have on three people who loved him dearly – his mum, dad and younger sister, Claire. 'I know he would never, ever hurt us. Just a fortnight before he died, I remember he said, "Mum, one thing I know is that you love me."'

In the aftermath of Garry's death, the family had to draw on every reserve of strength they had to keep going. 'When something like this happens, you either sink or swim.' After Garry's death, they discovered that there was no easily accessible bereavement support available for families in their situation. In the hope of preventing other suicides, they decided to share their story and say, 'this happened to our child and we're going to talk about it', thereby bringing the issue into the public arena.

'You won't prevent every suicide but we must start asking questions as to how to stop the high incidence, especially among young men. There must be something that can be done.' Rev. Dr Tony Byrne, a community worker with extensive experience in the area of suicide, says that one of the best ways of dealing with grief is, in your own time, to start helping others. Indeed, Mary and John have dedicated themselves to trying to assist other families who have been through a similar tragedy and to trying to reduce the number of families who have to go through it at all.

Still, Mary says it doesn't get any easier: 'We're getting on with things, but it's still devastating. We are just trying to get the bits together as best we can. Garry is the last thing I think of at night and the first thing I think of in the morning. I talk to him and pray for him.' Since the day he was buried, Mary has found it too hard to return to her son's grave. 'I couldn't handle it.' Mary says her daughter, Claire, is great. 'She goes to the grave every three days and waters the flowers. Garry and Claire were very close.' When Garry died it was very hard for his younger sister, but Mary says she is doing really well now. 'She's just going into her Leaving Cert year.'

Mary is reminded of Garry by everything in the house. 'In his room, I see the bed, the CD collection and I have to get out of there. The table in the house is still set for four and then we have to take his chair away. He used to change the time on my phone for me. I go to ask him to do it and he isn't there. I still have his number on my phone. I am totally heart-broken, but you have to get on with your lives.'

The inquest into Garry's death was held in October, nine months after he died. 'It was a rough, rough day. We had to sit and listen to a couple of road traffic accident deaths and one or two other suicides.' Mary sat in a daze, not listening, until she heard Garry's name called out. 'Hearing the finer details was very hard. My husband, John, had to go up and give evidence. We had to go through all that, and then there was the rigmarole of it being in the papers. As a mother, it was very hard – devastating and horrific.' There was a long wait for the inquest, which prolonged the torture. 'If it had been a month, it would have been better.' Mary says the family received great support from the local Garda. 'He came with us and he was very good to us.'

Throughout the interview, Mary tries to remain composed, but when she remembers the times with Garry before he died, she finds it very hard. She eventually breaks down completely as she remembers her beloved son when he was just a baby. 'When you remember your child as a little baby, suicide is something you never imagine will ever happen. You don't see this coming. John and I had two children and we did the best we could for them. I always thought Garry would be around when I was old. I'm purely heartbroken with Garry not around.'

The day that Garry was found dead, Mary received a visit from neighbour Cáit Kerins (who had lost her brother to suicide in 2000), offering to provide a listening ear. When neighbour Kevin Fallon died by suicide months after Garry, it was Mary McTernan who provided a listening ear to her.

The deaths of three young men aged between 24 and 27 in only four and a half years made the three families realise that suicide was a serious problem; they decided that they wanted to do something about it. So, Cáit Kerins, Carmel Fallon and Mary came together with other families in October 2004 to set up a small committee, with the aim of organising a conference to bring the issue out into the open.

STOP organised its first conference for February 2005. Seven hundred people from all over Ireland turned up to the conference;

many of those were people who had been bereaved and who had not found an outlet for their grief or a place to talk about their loss prior to the conference. Bereaved families and, indeed, individuals who had thought about suicide were drawn to the conference and travelled hundreds of miles to find a forum to learn more about the issue. Some conference delegates who had lost people to suicide told of how they had not spoken about their loss for longer than a decade, owing to the stigma surrounding it. STOP has received numerous calls from people in crisis since the conference – from parents whose child has made an attempt on their life and from people who have actually attempted it themselves. 'We have received calls from all over Ireland, from people who are suffering from depression to people who are having relationship problems.'

When Garry died, the McTernans attended a couple of counselling sessions, which they found of immense benefit. The McTernan family talks a lot about Garry and his suicide. They find that talking among themselves and also with friends helps a lot.

STOP organises group sessions, where bereaved families can come in and talk about their child in groups. 'We have three facilitators. Myself, Carmel and Cáit are all trained.' STOP now has a list of families from all around the country who want to come and talk. Mary refers callers on to their GPs, the Samaritans or Aware depending on the nature of the call.

'We felt that suicide was a hidden issue which still had a stigma attached. Suicide is just "put away". Between January 2004 and August 2005, there have been at least nine suicides in Co. Leitrim. If there were nine road traffic accidents, there would be a public outcry. There are huge campaigns for drink-driving and speeding, and rightly so, but suicide remains hidden. Just 7 per cent of the health budget goes to tackling suicide. Through education and public awareness, the STOP organisation hopes to curb the massive suicide rate nationally.'

If you have lost someone close to you, especially through suicide, and would like to talk to STOP, you can contact Mary McTernan on 071 9164286 or by email at stopsuicide@eircom.net.

Kevin Fallon

Kevin Fallon was 25 when he died on 30 May 2004. His mother, Carmel, believes that Kevin had experienced a tremendous amount of loss in his life owing to difficulties surrounding access to his daughter. Carmel thinks that this was instrumental in his decision to take his life.

Carmel is one of the three founders of the STOP organisation in Co. Leitrim and she feels very strongly about the importance of people being able to talk about their problems. 'The opposite of expression is depression.' I initially met Carmel in February 2005, when she appeared on *The Late Late Show*, along with co-founders of STOP, Mary McTernan and Cáit Kerins, to highlight the subject of suicide.

We met again in Leitrim about 15 months after Kevin had died and, though her grief was still very raw, Carmel was very open and honest with me. As with all of the families who have shared their experiences with me for this book, Carmel was anxious to share Kevin's story, hoping that it may inform and help others and, at some point, save another mother from the trauma that she has gone through and will continue to go through for the rest of her life. Her voice was steady throughout the interview, but when we talked about the way Kevin once was and the day her beloved son died, it all came flooding back and Carmel found it hard to hold back the tears.

'Kevin was always full of life. He was a lovely-looking fella.' The big problem in Kevin's life concerned his little daughter. 'He had a little girl but wasn't with her mother anymore and the child was with her mother. Kevin looked for custody of the child and was always coming and going out of the courts.'

Kevin later got involved in another relationship, which did not work out, and, through the courts, he did get access to his daughter one day a week and every other Sunday. Carmel describes the joy on Kevin's face when his little girl came into the room. 'He would light up when his child walked through the door.' She says that the main topic of conversation on Kevin's lips was always his daughter. 'What he spoke about was his child.' Carmel feels that the way her son was treated by the courts was a clear indication that custody battles usually favour women. 'The courts don't favour men. Although a lot of men run away from their responsibilities, Kevin didn't.'

Kevin spent two and a half years fighting on and off for access to his child. Inevitably, on a practical and emotional level, this took its toll and had a huge effect on his life. 'He worked as a plasterer in the same firm as his dad, but had to leave due to the pressure of trying to help his daughter. He was in and out of work.' At one stage, Carmel says Kevin hadn't seen his daughter for a long period and began to worry that she wouldn't recognise her dad the next time she saw him.

Before he died, things did seem to be looking up for Kevin. He had managed to hold down his job and was even building a house, but Carmel says that he had no peace of mind. 'After his child was taken away from him and from his home, Kevin never spent another night there until his reamins were brought there. He had a few drinks the night he died – we don't know how many.'

Kevin was the fourth boy in a family of eight. There were five boys and three girls. 'There was huge love between all of us and he got huge support from his family,' but Carmel says there was no warning that he was planning to take drastic steps to end his pain. 'He didn't tell you everything.'

Carmel was at work the day her son took his life. She got a few phone calls to say something terrible was wrong and the family was up at the hospital, but she didn't want to know. She rang another son on his mobile. 'All I could hear was crying on the phone.' Knowing that she was about to hear something terrible, Carmel switched off the phone. 'I knew something big was wrong and when they rang back, I wouldn't answer it. I stuck my fingers in my ears and walked around and around in work.' Still, Carmel knew that she could not postpone hearing about the bad news forever and so she rang a friend to bring her up to the hospital.

'I arrived at the hospital and I saw my husband. I knew something terrible was wrong, but nobody had actually said that someone was dead. I was clinging on to hope.' Carmel walked up to her husband and she just said, 'It's Kevin, isn't it? Suicide?' Carmel says that once she heard that something was wrong, deep down she knew it was Kevin, but she couldn't acknowledge it at first. Carmel had seen her son's pain and her intuition told her that the bad news concerned Kevin. 'I knew all the stuff he had been through. There's a breaking point for everyone. He was always talking about the child. It had been going on for three years at this stage. Kevin loved that child, but he was up against a brick wall.'

The day before Kevin died, he had been working with his dad and that evening he was linesman at a football match. He sold tickets for a GAA raffle and then went to the pub. 'My husband found him hanging the next morning. His dad took him down. He died at about 6.30 in the morning.'

Carmel says the whole family knew it was difficult for Kevin, but they had no idea it had got so bad. He had spoken to both his father and his sister on the day he died, but he didn't tell them anything. Carmel says the family doesn't torture itself asking, *Why?* 'We don't ask *Why?* I've never been guilty. I have been a good, supportive, responsible mother. Kevin was my sixth child. I did my best. Everything was not hunky dory and grandeur, but there was huge love. He was heartbroken about the child and he did say to us, "You don't understand."'

Carmel thinks of Kevin every day of her life. She has nothing left of her young son except mementoes and her memories of him. 'I have loads of stuff that Kevin gave me – little pressies; he would always buy pressies.' Carmel starts to cry as she casts her mind over those precious reminders of Kevin's kindness and generosity. 'He was great, he had so much love to give. He was always getting pressies for his nieces and nephews.'

She manages a smile again as she remembers Kevin's great sense of fun. 'He was full of life, full of craic. He was always bringing animals around to the house. He loved playing games.' She laughs as she tells me how Kevin once moved a 'For Sale' sign and placed it outside a friend's house. 'He had a lot of friends. He played football and had a lot of young ones involved in football. He loved children and always minded his cousins. Kevin lived a very full life. We loved him and still love him. I think of my son last thing at night and first thing in the morning. I think of him thousands of times during the day.'

'I'm okay some days, other days it's like a big tonne weight. It will always be there. I don't want any other family to have to go through what I've gone through as a mother.' Since his death, Carmel has done up the whole house, including Kevin's bedroom, but has been unable to throw away his clothes. 'I've kept his clothes. I haven't washed the clothes he was wearing that night.' Carmel says it was a long time after Kevin's death before she was able to look at any of his stuff. It was pretty devastating to see that a mortgage had just come through for Kevin three days before he died.

'Some days I'm good, but other days I'm not so good. Some days I wouldn't mind dying. Nobody ever intends to bring a child into the world for that pain and suffering. It was the circumstances. It was the losses.' Carmel gets very upset when she reflects on the immense hurt of losing her beloved son. 'It's a very rough deal. I'm 53 now ... I have prayed, lit candles, said rosaries – prayed and prayed. I've to deal with it myself. You need to tell [people about] it. People need to know.'

Carmel is determined to shatter the silence surrounding suicide. 'Nothing has been done because people are hiding it. I know I'm a strong woman and I can and will talk about it, but there are people who can't handle the fact that their loved one died in such a way.' Carmel wants to see a nationwide programme introduced with the aim of showing young people that suicide is not their only option. This is something that a lot of people in the area of suicide prevention feel is of utmost importance. 'I want something in schools so they can deal with the ups and downs of what life throws at them and not be afraid to talk about it, to be able to speak about it. The other academic subjects would come easily after that. I want to see a programme in place for young people in schools, a programme to have them express themselves. It's my one dream.'

'Regardless of jobs, houses and how we relate to others, we need to get in touch with ourselves and the reality. If you can't say what's in your hearts, education and other things have no meaning. Never mind reaching for the stars, we need to have our feet on the ground. People don't have time for each other. It's all rush, rush, rush … and work. Kevin was rushing, too. There is lots of time. Let's use it in effective ways and stop worrying about money. People have lost touch with spirituality. Life has become focused on power and property. People may be better off financially, but worse off in another sense.'

Carmel says that the problem of suicide continues to grow. 'While suicide is being swept under the carpet, the problem is growing and growing. Silence is feeding it. I came home one day and my daughter told me about another guy who had killed himself, then another – it's continuing to happen. I know I'm not going to stop every suicide. There will always be suicide, but the numbers can certainly be reduced. Something has to be done [about] all of this.'

Neighbours Mary and John McTernan and Cáit Kerins, who also lost family members to suicide, were there for Carmel. She says it makes such a difference when you actually have someone there who understands – she says that out of this understanding has come the motivation for STOP, the organisation they set up in February 2005 to help others bereaved by suicide and to reduce the stigma around it.

'A lot more needs to be done. We need to keep talking about it, we need to keep it out there, keep requesting that some project be put in place. We need to think about how people are feeling and who can they talk to when they have a problem.'

Carmel feels that if they can save just one person's life through STOP, it will be worth it. 'We have to get young people talking.' Carmel wants to see the stigma reduced and she hates to hear stories of people pretending their loved one's death was an accident when it was actually suicide.

Pat Kerins

Cáit Kerins lost her brother Pat to suicide in November 2000. She provided support to the McTernan family when Garry died and later came into contact with Carmel Fallon when Kevin died. They decided to take action in the hope of preventing other families from suffering the terrible grief they have gone through and continue to struggle with. Conferences such as the STOP conference, as well as seminars and research on the subject of suicide, continue to explore and highlight the problem to a wider audience.

The willingness of those tragically bereaved by suicide to talk openly about the subject at seminars and in the media gives tremendous courage and assistance to those who have lost loved ones to suicide and who have, in the past, been silenced by the stigma. Thanks to the tremendous work of the Irish Association of Suicidology (IAS) and the Trojan work carried out by voluntary organisations, that stigma has been significantly reduced in recent years and the government has been forced to sit up and take notice. Still, government funding into suicide prevention is seen as constituting a drop in the ocean. President of the IAS, Dan Neville TD, pointed out in 2005 that the government had spent a meagre €17 million on suicide prevention since the National Task Force on Suicide reported in 1998. He argued that the low levels of funding intended to deal with the rates of suicide amounted to neglect, saying that the stigma associated with suicide is obstructing it from being the subject of a nationwide prevention campaign.

In September 2005, at the launch of 'Reach Out, the National Strategy for Action on Suicide Prevention 2005–2014', I had a chat with Dan Neville TD. I asked him whether the new National Office for Suicide Prevention and the additional €500,000 funding, along with a promise of further budget allocations over the coming years, gave him any confidence. He didn't look very hopeful, telling me that there had been no significant movement on state strategy since the 1998 National Task Force. He told me that the latest strategy held many recommendations similar to those of 1998. He hopes to see those strategies put into action instead of simply put on paper.

Cáit Kerins hopes that through the STOP organisation she can use her experience of losing her brother Pat to help others in similar situations and break the wall of silence. Attending the conference in the Abbey Manor Hotel in Dromahair, Co. Leitrim in February 2005, I was stunned by the significant number of people who informed me that they had lost people to suicide and, owing to the stigma, had not known where to go. Some even said that they had never spoken about their loved one's death prior to coming to the conference. The stigma surrounding suicide has lessened significantly in recent years, with national media coverage on the issue appearing a number of times a week. Though many working in the area of suicide prevention say that there is still a huge amount of work to be done to reduce the stigma, Ireland has made huge progress.

Cáit feels that by sharing experiences, strength and hope, the confusion will be confronted. 'Hiding behind the stigma attached to suicide must end.'

Cáit was very close to her brother Pat and his death by suicide in November 2000, at the age of just 27, was a tremendous shock. Pat came fourth in a family of six boys and two girls. Cáit says he was always in great form, bubbly, happy and always on for a laugh. 'If I was ever worried, he would be the one to say to me "what will it matter in a few months time or a year's time?"' Pat was a builder by trade, working for a local man in the town of Dromahair. The timing of his death coincided with him taking a week off work. 'He was owed a week's holidays and he said, "Sure why not take them now?"'

The Monday and Tuesday of that week, Cáit says her brother was as normal as ever. 'On the Wednesday he spent all day in bed, complaining that he was sick with a head cold. I found that very strange.' That evening, however, he went out with his first cousin for something to eat. 'They had the usual craic and there was nothing different about Pat.' The following day Pat was working on the family farm, where he regularly helped his dad.

At about one o'clock that day, Pat came into the house. His mum was looking for a lift into Dromahair. 'Pat wanted to bring her in on the tractor – she got a lift instead!' His behaviour that day was completely normal. 'He cooked himself egg and chips that afternoon [...] The two of us were up in the house and he was excited about his young nephew [who had started] walking.' At one point, Pat stared at Cáit in a strange way, but before she could ask him what it was about he smiled at her and the moment was forgotten. Then, at about 1.45 pm, one of Pat's very good friends dropped over to ask Pat to go to the mart with him. Pat said he had things to do so he wouldn't go, but he made his friend a cup of tea and the two chatted for a while at the table. Cáit knew Pat had bales of hay to move from one shed to another, so there was still nothing out of the ordinary in his behaviour.

The family have pieced together the final hours before Pat's death from people who saw him that day. 'At 3 o'clock, he got on his tractor. He gave my next-door neighbour a big wave. About 3.20, another friend of Pat's came along. Pat was leaning across the gate, having a cigarette. His friend noticed that the tractor was facing up the lane. He finished his fag and told his friend that he had to go. That same friend was coming back at about 4.20. The tractor was reversed up to the gate and the cows were all looking into the shed.'

It was dinner time when the Kerins family would first wonder where Pat had got to. 'At about a quarter to five, mum had dinner ready and asked my brother Francis to go over to get Pat. He went over on the motorbike. It was dark by the time that he got to the lane and he went as far as the tractor and called to Pat to see was he all right.' When Francis heard no response, he called out again, and eventually went into the shed to find his brother dead, hanging from a beam on the ceiling. Stunned, Francis walked over to Pat and stood there for a few minutes, taking it all in. Francis then ran to the bottom of the road, unable to believe what he had just seen. 'He thought he must be seeing things.' Francis went back into the shed again and touched his brother – Pat was still warm.

It was shortly after a quarter to five when Francis found him and the family figures he must have died at about half-past four. Certain now that Pat was dead, Francis ran down to the end of the road again and rang his mother's phone. The moments and hours that followed were horrific for the family as each person learned what had happened, realised that others had to be informed, and then had to watch their loved ones take in the devastating reality. Cáit was in the bathroom when Francis's call came. She heard her mother scream and ran straight out to her. 'I met her in the hallway. She literally threw the phone at me and said, "Pat's dead. He hanged himself."' Cáit took the phone from her mother and Francis asked her to come over to him straight away. 'He said, "Pat's dead. I'm on my own."' Cáit grabbed her cigarettes and her mobile phone and ran out to the road and began to run down to where Francis was, a mile and a half away from the house. Francis was only 21 at the time. Cáit realised it would take too long to run the distance to the shed and decided to hitch. All she could think of was getting to Francis as quickly as possible. Luckily, her uncle was coming that way and Cáit stopped him and told him what had happened.

They quickly drove to where Francis was waiting and though her brother tried to stop her, she ran to the shed and saw Pat. 'I couldn't cry. I was just screaming. They probably heard me down in Dromahair.' As she took in the reality of what had just happened, Cáit went with Francis to the end of the road. The two just sat in a wet hedge, trying to absorb the shock. Then, other family members started to arrive, as well as the Gardaí, the priest and the GP. Cáit was wondering why Pat had still not been cut down and decided to go and get a knife, but the Gardaí came over and told her that no member of the family could cut him down or it would have to be treated as a crime scene.

The GP pronounced Pat dead and cut him down. 'We then had to wait for the coffin and the hearse to arrive.' In the middle of it all, their mother arrived at the scene. Their next-door neighbour had seen her walking along in the dark and had brought her over. Her mother wanted to go into the shed but the Gardaí talked her out of it. Their father still had to be informed. Cáit's fiancé, whom she has since married, drove her towards Boyle to meet her father. They met him about half a mile down the road. 'Dad had seen the police cars and thought a cow had broken loose.' Cáit's younger sister told their father. 'It looked like my dad literally sank into his boots, he flopped down the road and fell into my mother's arms.' Pat was brought away in a hearse to the morgue and the family followed behind.

Once the initial shock was over, the nightmare continued. 'The *why's*? started. We were a very close family and all got on very well. I had heard about suicides happening in the past, but never believed it could happen to us. My mum was absolutely shattered and shocked and stunned. Daddy was the same. I didn't sleep for the first month. I hated the evenings when 10 o'clock came. I would start cleaning and keep going until 5 or 6 am. I was so frightened of the dark. Once Mum and Dad got up, then I would go to bed for two or three hours.'

'The boys were angry, so was [my sister] Mary Teresa. I just thought whatever pain he was going through, he'd taken with him.' Still, the pain of bereavement was tremendous: 'It's as if someone had reached into your body and taken half of you. It rips a family apart, but can also bring them closer together. It would only take one person in the family to bring everyone down. If you came in and your mother was crying, everyone would start crying. A loved one is gone, your own flesh and blood took his own life, he couldn't talk to you. If you get a good day – take it.'

The inquest was horrendous. Cáit says the family had to sit through ten detailed descriptions of other deaths, including car accidents. This is a common problem that families who have lost someone to suicide feel needs changing and is dealt with in another chapter of this book. Cáit doesn't know why the result couldn't be delivered privately to the family in one room, instead of in front of a courtroom full of people. 'It's the last thing you need.'

For the first two years after Pat's death, the family kept asking, 'What if?'. 'You could be having a great day and it would just hit you like that and then you'd cry for the rest of the day. I'd go to his grave and talk to him. On New Year's Eve, I went up to Pat's grave and wished him a Happy New Year. I'd tell Pat about my day. "Why did you do it Pat? You've to help us be happy." All of us go to the grave. I'd often ring Dad from Sligo and ask him to come and pick me up. I felt as if I had to be at home all the time. I felt that I wanted to be there for my parents. I couldn't even spend an hour in my fiancé's house. I rallied around after my brothers – I was worried about them.'

Every time the family hears of another suicide, their mood sinks as they think of the other family. 'Forever, not a day goes past that I don't think of Pat. I don't go to the shed since that terrible evening. I wanted to burn the shed. I blamed the shed, but you can't take it out on the shed. You do get the strength to go on; you get the strength to smile again. Even in the last year, I've seen how the family has come on. My wedding last year, though it was a sad day, it was a good day. Pat was supposed to be one of the groomsmen.'

Looking back, Cáit says they realise that there were signs. 'He had gone on a shopping trip to Sligo and bought loads of clothes for himself. A short while afterwards, he gave them all away to the boys.' Giving treasured personal possessions away is one of the warning signs of suicide (see Chapter 25 – Warning Signs of Suicide). However, as Cáit says, though she had heard of suicides in the past, they never believed it could happen to one of their family members and, like most of the population, they never dreamt that they would need to be aware of the warning signs. Cáit also believes that the look Pat gave her the day he died was another sign, but a look can mean a thousand things and there is no warning look to indicate that someone is planning to take their lives. Though warning signs can be indicators that someone may be planning to take their lives, many are extremely subtle and could easily have an alternative explanation. People may give their clothes away if they are the wrong size, if they are planning a trip to the States to buy low-cost designer clothes or for numerous other reasons. Warning signs must be viewed in context.

Another possible indicator that something was amiss was the fact that Pat had lost weight. Cáit explains, 'I had only really realised that about two weeks before he died. When I mentioned it to him, he said, "Better to be thin than fat"', so clearly Cáit saw no reason for concern. Pat had also asked his sister Mary Teresa what colour her wedding dress was going to be. She had said, 'White, why?' Mary Teresa was the first in the family to get married. 'My cousin had commented that the wedding would be a fantastic day and Pat had said, "Sure, God knows where we'll be."' In the context of Pat's suicide, the family, looking back, now believes that Pat knew he wasn't going to be around for his sister's wedding. Cáit now feels that Pat knew exactly what he was doing. Pat also made some funny comments such as 'if I kick the bucket, make sure to put 20 fags in with me.' Cáit also found loads of cigarette butts in his bedroom after he died and knew that this meant that he hadn't been sleeping. She says she hates to think of what he must have been going through.

Since losing her brother, Cáit has done a huge amount of research into understanding suicide and depression and says she wishes she had known then what she knows now, as there were a number of warning signs in her brother's behaviour.

Although Cáit now believes that Pat had been planning his suicide for a while, on the surface he appeared fine. Pat's life and mood seemed to be great in the lead-up to his death. 'He had no serious girlfriend, but loads of friends. He loved GAA and would always go to the pub to watch the All-Ireland Final. He was always out for a few drinks and we would all be together for different family occasions – 21st birthdays and holidays. He had cattle, money, sheep – he had even bought a car two weeks before he died. He hadn't been to the doctor. Everything was going well for him and we would have assumed that if he had a problem, he would have come and talked to us.'

Cáit says that initially they had no idea where to get help. 'There was nobody to tell me where to go for help. Neighbours and friends were brilliant. We did talk about it at home.' There was a huge funeral. Fr John McTernan, who had come to the scene, also came and did prayers and songs in the house. 'It was a big comfort to the family. None of us got counselling at the time.'

Cáit took it upon herself to look after the rest of the family and kept encouraging them all to get counselling. She says some of her brothers wouldn't talk about it and every time Pat's name was mentioned they would change the subject.

Eventually, worrying about them all took its toll on Cáit and she found herself at a very low ebb. She sought help and tried to get counselling. She was told she would have to wait a minimum of three months, which she says is totally unacceptable. She says someone who needs help cannot wait three months.

Cáit attended lectures by Rev. Dr Tony Byrne and learned the warning signs of suicide and also about what she was going through herself. She had had a lump in her throat for months and, on learning that this was one of the many symptoms of bereavement, it went away.

'Once a woman said to me, "Time's a healer." I thought she was mad at the time, but it does get easier. At birthdays, on anniversaries and at Christmas now, we're starting to say, "Remember Pat".' The pain has lessened somewhat and Cáit has learned to cope better. 'I'm not as protective. I've learned to let go. The boys are fine. When I moved out of Mum and Dad's in 2004, I kept thinking "how will they survive without me?", but you learn to let go. It does get easier. The first three years are particularly hard. I know it's like that with any death, but what is particularly hard is the fact that Pat died on his own and it's painful to think about what his last thoughts must have been.'

Now Cáit can smile when she remembers her brother. She believes you have to appreciate the light-hearted moments and recalls the Gardaí arriving to the scene of Pat's death. They had difficulty getting up to the shed because of the wet land and they literally had to stop vans driving by in the hope of getting a pair of wellies.

'There were two Garda cars and cars kept stopping to see what was going on. We managed to get a pair of wellies. Then, the priest arrived and he had no wellies, so we had to stop another van to get another pair of wellies. We still have a pair of wellies in the shed to this day and we don't know who owns them.'

In May 2004, Cáit approached Mary and John McTernan about doing something about the problem of suicide. They set up what started as a little group, with a view to organising a seminar. Only weeks later, they learned of another neighbour's suicide, 25-year-old year Kevin, and offered whatever help they could. The three families realised that their three young sons had all died by suicide in such a tiny area over just four and a half years. They realised that something had to be done, not only to raise awareness of the problem of suicide, but also to work towards reducing the stigma attached to it and to try to help the many families in Ireland bereaved by suicide, who, just like Cáit, didn't know where to go for help. The three met in Dromahair and established the STOP organisation (Suicide, Teach, Organise, Prevent) and organised their first conference for February 2005.

Shortly before the conference, the three – Mary McTernan, Cáit Kerins and Carmel Fallon – appeared on *The Late Late Show* to highlight the issue of suicide and to share their stories. The tremendous response they received directly after the show indicated that there were a lot of people out there in agony over the loss of a loved one to suicide, people who needed to learn more in order to understand the torture they were going through. The conference was booked out immediately and hundreds of people from all over Ireland made the journey to Dromahair for the two-day event.

The opening talks by Rev. Dr Tony Byrne and Sr Kathleen Maguire on the causes of suicide, long-term intervention and prevention and the journey through grief provided visible comfort and the beginnings of comprehension for many families, many of whom were attending such a conference for the first time ever. Rev. Dr Tony Byrne urged those bereaved to try to pick up their lives and suggested that one of the greatest ways of dealing with grief is, in your own good time, to help others. 'Don't allow yourselves to increase the blame. You would have done all you could to protect your loved one if you could.'

Rev. Dr Tony Byrne told those bereaved by suicide that they bore no responsibility for the deaths of their loved ones by suicide, discussing the notion of 'diminished responsibility' associated with a suicidal person.

STOP continues to highlight the problem of suicide and in 2005, it formed links with a number of similar organisations around Ireland with the aim of establishing an All-Ireland approach to suicide prevention among voluntary organisations. At the time of going to print, STOP told me that the first 'Bereaved by Suicide' session was up and running.

Sharon

A lot of media reporting on suicide tends to focus around men, which is not surprising with nearly 80 per cent of all of people who die by suicide being male. Still, out of a total of 457 deaths by suicide in 2004, 101 were females and figures amongst young women are on the increase. Since 1980, the overall rate of female suicide has not increased; however, the rate of suicide in young women aged between 15 and 24 more than doubled in the 1990s. Recent provisional data suggests that the female overall rate may be increasing.

Paul from Console, the Bereaved by Suicide Foundation, lost his 22-year-old sister, Sharon, to suicide in 2001. He still can't understand for a moment the reasoning behind Sharon's drastic decision and his eyes are filled with sadness and love when he remembers her.

As in a number of the stories in this book, Sharon was the baby of the family. 'There were ten of us. We were a big, Dublin family. Sharon was the baby and we all loved her and spoiled her.' Because there was such a gap in age between Sharon and the rest of the family, there was 'fierce excitement' when she was born.

As a child she was deeply loved – her sisters took her under their wing. Meanwhile, she had big brothers who were crazy about her and who were always looking out for her. Viewing Sharon's life from different perspectives, she appeared to have everything going for her. She was successful and fortunate on all fronts and seemed to be very happy. Throughout her school years, she was busy and involved in a lot of different activities. Sharon was very into sport and music and was also very creative. 'She was good at guitar and art and was very bright academically.' She had plenty of friends and Paul says she was very popular in school. Furthermore, as a high achiever, she would often win awards and was constantly being recognised. 'We were all very proud of her. It was always a celebration with Sharon. We'd celebrate her successes in debating, in sport – everything.'

At university, Sharon's life continued to go really well. She was very interested in the humanities and chose to study sociology. 'She was a girl who loved people and had lots of friends. You'd come out and there would be a crowd in the kitchen. She was always off for weekends with friends overseas.' On the romantic front, Sharon had many admirers and had had boyfriends. 'We were a very close-knit family. Our family was full of hugs and Mum kept us all very close together. There were the normal tiffs, but we were always there for each other. There was a nice secure feeling in our home. We were all healthy and had a happy childhood and never had any major problems.'

Sharon came out of college with an excellent degree and was offered a top job in a multinational company based in Dublin. She decided, however, that she wanted to travel the world first with a group of friends. 'Herself and her friends decided they were going off for a year, around Asia, and she took a year off from her job.' As the youngest, Sharon was well looked after by all of her older siblings, as well as her parents. Her mum brought her to the travel agency to book her flights and her brothers and sisters organised money for her. 'She was very excited.' Sharon would never take that trip: little did her adoring family know at the time that their baby sister was planning to take her life.

A couple of nights before she was due to head off, she went out with friends from work. 'She dropped into Mum that night, dressed up beautifully. As she was leaving the house, she said to Mum, "You know I love you, don't you?" and she threw her arms around Mum. Later, she rang Mum from the restaurant.' Later again, she rang from the pub she was in. 'She rang twice that night and kept saying, "I love you, Mum".'

Paul was in work the next morning. His job involved travelling and he was out on business in the car when his phone rang. 'It was a Garda. He asked me who I was and did I have a sister called Sharon. He asked could I meet him at Blanchardstown hospital, but he wouldn't say why.' Immediately worried, Paul went straight to the hospital, where he was greeted by an unmarked Garda car; his mother was in the back seat. One of the Gardaí got out of the car and approached Paul. He said, 'I've bad news for you. Your sister Sharon is dead and we suspect it's suicide.' The Gardaí had not yet told Paul's mother – all that she knew at this stage was that it was something about her daughter. 'The Gardaí handled it well. They were wonderful.' Paul's father was away at work at the time and they were unable to contact him.

Paul was faced with the horrendous task of having to go in and identify his sister's body. He went into denial, unable to accept that his beloved sister, who was so close to him, had done something so final and drastic. 'I went in and identified my sister. She had taken a cocktail of tablets and drink. When I went in, she was still fresh in her clothes. I went into a state of shock, trying to wake her up, begging her, taking her in my arms and holding her, trying to wake her up, my little, beautiful sister.' The whole family was about to be destroyed. Paul's mother still didn't know that Sharon was dead and Paul now had to face telling his mother that her little baby was dead, her little daughter, and to make it worse, he had to tell her that she had died by suicide.

Paul brought his mother in. 'I'll never forget the screams. It was like a wounded animal, a primal cry, as she tried to bring her daughter back to life. She was very close to her. The two of them used to go shopping together. Sharon kept my mother young.'

Sharon died on 17 October 2001. As the other members of the family were informed about the tragedy, they each came to the hospital. The whole family was in total shock. First, they had to try to take in the enormity of what had happened, realising in that tragic moment that life and the family would never be the same again for any of them. The biggest shock was that Sharon had chosen to do it.

'It was the element of choice, the fact that our sister had decided to take her own life.'

The bewilderment and disbelief felt by all intensified as they learned that Sharon must have been planning her death for a while. 'She had left letters for each of us, we don't know how long before she knew what she going to do. As a brother, I felt I failed her. She was obviously in crisis to do what she did, for her to choose to end her life. There had to be something seriously wrong, because our instinct is to survive.' Paul comments on how strongly people normally cling to life in so many situations, referring to people in hospices and during 9/11.

Paul had always been very close to Sharon and couldn't believe she didn't come to him with whatever problems she may have been having. 'In my mind, I thought, "Sharon, we were very close. You told me about the break-up in your relationship, things you couldn't tell Mum."' Paul is convinced that Sharon had to have some problem, one that hadn't been diagnosed and was well-hidden. 'There were no apparent signs of depression. She was so gregarious, so full of life, great socially – she loved people. She always had a tremendous capacity to live and achieved and accomplished a lot.'

The funeral was packed and, to add to the family's grief, the parish priest announced to the congregation that he didn't condone what had happened. 'It was harrowing. We were devastated and in shock. I knew there and then that Mum wouldn't survive it. Afterwards, Mum kept going to Sharon's grave and she kept crying.'

The toll Sharon's death would take on the family made for further devastation. Paul recalls how his mother, who was in her late sixties at the time, fell apart. 'My mother was a very dynamic woman, an incredible woman, with a great sense of humour, but this all changed when Sharon died. Mum couldn't come to terms with the loss of her little baby. We tried to help her, but she died within six months of Sharon. We wanted to protect Mum, but she neglected herself and stopped eating. She just wanted to die. She just wanted to be with Sharon, her daughter. I loved Mum and miss her terribly. She died of a broken heart. She was always a bit of a mother-hen, who loved her grandchildren, and loved a few social drinks.'

When Paul's father lost his life partner as well as his baby daughter, he too gave up. 'He didn't want to live – he stopped looking after himself. He wasn't eating. Daddy died, pining [for] my sister and my mother. He had a massive stroke at the age of 69. My mother died of something to do with her heart, but we knew she died of a broken heart – as a family, we are fully aware of that.'

In the space of little more than 12 months, Paul lost his sister, his mother and his father. The rest of the family were mostly married at the time of Sharon's death. Paul's children adored Sharon. 'It had a terrible impact on their lives.' Paul's eyes fill with tears when he speaks of his beloved sister and recalls the happy times with Sharon and the rest of his family. Luckily, the family were very close, which Paul sees as a gift from his parents. 'The family was able to talk about Sharon after she died. We were very open with each other.'

None of the family had had any inkling of what Sharon was planning to do; there were no warning signs. 'We would almost have preferred if there were. If she had a history of psychiatric illness or if there were some explanation, at least, that [would have] made sense.' Instead, Sharon seemed to have everything going for her, especially for a girl of her age. 'She had money, a car, she was beautiful, great academically, was a great communicator and the whole family felt she was destined for great things. She was sharp and was able to speak her mind, and great at arguing.' Sharon was also widely regarded as great fun; she had a wicked, caustic sense of humour and a very friendly disposition.

She died in her rented apartment in Dublin, where she lived with friends. She was found by a friend of hers and she had left a number of letters in the apartment for her loved ones. 'She had obviously planned her suicide because, that particular night, she knew her flatmates would be away.' The family don't even know whether she had ever planned to go on the trip to Asia. The trip had been planned for a couple of months and the girls she was supposed to travel with were shocked and devastated when Sharon took her life a couple of days before they were to set off together.

The family still goes to the grave to visit, but they are left with no answers. It was very hard for Paul to walk down a corridor and tell his mother that her daughter was dead. Paul also had to tell the other members of the family what had happened.

Paul feels now that his sister must have been in crisis. He and the rest of the family, like all families bereaved by suicide, kept asking *Why?* and asked themselves whether they could have prevented it. 'Did we fail her? We were filled with guilt, wondering did we fail her, and a sense of loss. I was angry with her at times myself and would ask: "Why did you do this?"'

The feelings of anger went away very quickly for them. 'At the end of the day, I had lost my little sister. Sharon was brave, sensitive and loving – a wonderful, caring human being.' Paul's mother was tortured with guilt. 'She blamed herself. My mother wanted answers; she wanted to know why. I brought her to a counsellor, who after two visits admitted that she was out of her depth when it came to suicide. She explained she was a bereavement counsellor, not specifically trained in suicide.'

The night Sharon died she left individual letters for the whole family and Paul's mother insisted that they were all read out. They spent hours trying to figure out why Sharon had chosen to take her life. The letters, all quite similar in style, stated that she knew that none of the family would be happy with her decision. 'She said she was sorry in the letter, but felt it was best for her.' There was no explanation offered. She indicated that she had made this decision and then she wrote about the relationship she had with the individual the letter was addressed to.

The family talked to everyone, looking for the slightest clue. 'We talked to her friends who were with her that night and asked what she was like in the hours coming up to her death. I met so many people who bumped into her that night. They all said she was in such high spirits.' It seemed that Sharon saw the night as a farewell. 'She had made a point of saying, "I love you" to Mum in the house and before she got into the car. It tortured my Mum.' Unusual, too, was something else Sharon did the day that she went with her Mum to book the tickets for her trip: 'When she came out [of the travel agency], she saw a beggar in the street and Sharon put a wad of notes into the beggar's hand. It was a bit unusual.' The family considered every possible issue that could have played a role in Sharon's decision to die by suicide. 'We considered all options. She was not the type who could be bullied [...] nothing added up.'

Paul says that Sharon always brought immense joy to the family and when she died, this was all turned upside down. 'It was horrendous, to have her taken away from you.' Sharon's inquest took place about eight months after her death. 'The Gardaí were very sensitive and looked after us well.' Still, the inquest was terrible for the family and they found it particularly hard to have to sit through the other cases, which included sudden deaths, road traffic accidents, murders and one other suicide. 'It was very rough.'

The pain of losing Sharon in such a terrible way will be with Paul and his family for the rest of their lives. Paul now wants to do as much as he can for others whose lives have been shattered by the loss of loved ones and he is one of the founding directors of Console, the Bereaved by Suicide Foundation. Console provides professional counselling and support services to those bereaved by suicide. They assist people who have lost a relative or friend to suicide and would like the comfort and understanding of others who have experienced a similar loss. Console also organises conferences and seminars to explore the subject and learn more about it and provides referrals to appropriate professionals for people in crisis. They also produce a selection of literature for those bereaved on the subject of living with suicide.

For further information, contact: Console – Bereaved by Suicide Foundation, All Hallows College, Grace Park Road, Drumcondra, Dublin 9.

Tel: (01) 857 4300

Helpline Tel: 1800 201 890

Email: info@console.ie

Web: www.console.ie

Teen-Line: The Story of Darren Bolger

In 1980, 27 young men aged between 15 and 24 died by suicide in Ireland. During the 1980s and 1990s this figure rose dramatically. By 1998, it had more than quadrupled – 118 young men in the 15–24 age bracket took their lives. Although the rate of suicide in Ireland has fallen slightly since it peaked in 1998, the rate among young people and particularly among young men remains worryingly high. The increase indicates that the pressures of modern society are taking their toll on young people. As suicide is nearly always a tremendous shock to the friends and family left behind, it raises many questions. Why are young people not talking about their problems or seeking help? Is there no-one they can turn to to discuss their problems?

Following the death by suicide of her 16-year-old son, Darren, Maureen Bolger from Tallaght decided to set up a phoneline for teenagers, where they could openly discuss any issues they had.

Maureen recalls the day in April 2003, when she saw 16-year-old Darren for the last time. The day had started out just like any other. Maureen was about to go out for a hair appointment as she was going to a 70th birthday party that evening. Darren was standing over by the counter-top in the kitchen and she asked him whether he was heading out that day. He said he was going to The Square shopping centre with his friend, as he often would, and, without giving the matter any further thought, Maureen said, 'See you later' and left. 'See you later, Mom,' Darren replied.

Normal family activity followed in the house and there was no indication whatsoever that Darren was planning something drastic. Maureen's partner, Eddie, as well as her sister and brother-in-law, were in the house and it was agreed that Eddie would make a big fry-up, on the condition that Darren washed up afterwards. Everyone was in great form and Darren had them all in fits of laughter throughout the meal. When they finished, Darren was about to walk out the door when he was stopped by Eddie, who reminded him that he still had dishes to wash. Darren's hand was in a cast, however, as he had been attacked by a group of youths in a nearby estate only six weeks before and, in defending himself, had damaged his knuckle. He held up his injured hand and grinned at Eddie, letting him know that it was impossible for him to do the washing-up, and off he went to join his friends in The Square. It was about midday. His friends say he was the 'usual Darren' at The Square, in top spirits and laughing and joking.

Maureen returned to the house later in the afternoon. Darren had come back home to change and had then gone over to his aunt's house to see his cousins. Maureen and Eddie headed off to the 70th birthday party. Again, everyone thought Darren was his usual good-humoured self: he was making up songs and joking with all his cousins. At about 12.25 that night, Maureen gave Darren a call just to check if he was staying with his friend, as he sometimes did, or if he would be staying at home. With the noise from the function, it was a little difficult to hear what Darren was saying, so Maureen got her partner, Eddie, to call Darren back. Darren told Eddie to tell his mother that he loved her, which was normal for Darren. 'He was always telling me he loved me.'

Still, Maureen had an uneasy feeling at the party. About 40 minutes later, she got a call from her son Alan. Alan told her to hurry home: something had happened to Darren. 'I jumped into a taxi and headed home.' Maureen didn't for a moment consider that her 16-year-old son could be dead, let alone that he could have taken his own life. 'The worst scenario I could imagine was that Darren may have been attacked by youths again and that they could have gone as far as to stab him – in the arm.'

By the time Maureen got back to the house, the ambulance had already been and gone, so Maureen went to the hospital. At this point, events became surreal for Maureen. She heard people say that the doctors were working on Darren, and there was some reference to him trying to take his own life. Maureen felt she was in a waking nightmare. The doctor came over to her and sat down beside her. She said she was sorry, that they had worked on Darren for nearly a full hour and they couldn't bring him back. The doctor herself was crying, but Maureen would not believe it. 'I felt Darren was fooling everyone. I said I'd go in and wake him up.'

Maureen went into the room where Darren was lying on the table. A candle was lighting and there was a sheet up as far as his neck. He had a little smile on his face and looked fast asleep. 'I kept saying, "Darren – wake up! You're my baby, you're my little pal," but he wouldn't answer me. I then said the phrase I [had] always said to him since he was about three: "I love you, Babye Faybe."' Darren didn't answer and the cold reality began to hit Maureen. 'I told him the joke was over, it wasn't funny any more, but he never got up.' The doctors tried to bring Maureen away. Darren's mother, her partner, Eddie, and his brothers, Alan and Anthony, were forced to accept that their beloved Darren, the 16-year-old baby of the family, had taken his own life.

The family was further bewildered when they discovered that Darren had been planning his death for four weeks and they hadn't picked up on the smallest sign. He had been in good form; there were no signs of depression. He had always been a motivated individual and the type who cheered others up when they were down. Darren was meticulous about his appearance and personal hygiene. He hadn't taken alcohol or drugs. He had left a suicide note, but it contained only messages of love for his family and no explanation. The note was addressed to the whole family and was written with his left hand as the right was in a cast. On the night he died, he did phone a lot of people; his last call was to his best friend and he left a message on the answering machine as it was quite late. Still, he gave no indication that there was anything wrong.

Even in hindsight, little things didn't really point to anything concrete. The fact that he gave his mother an Easter egg for Mother's day might have meant that he knew he wouldn't be around for Easter, but it's not unheard-of for people to give Easter eggs as gifts on other occasions. Maureen had even commented at the time that she must be the only mother getting an Easter egg on Mother's Day, but Darren had just smiled and said nothing. It was only a number of minor incidents, recalled after his death, that indicated that Darren had been planning his suicide for a full four weeks. He had idly asked a girl who was a friend of his whether she would cry for him if he died. Presuming that he was joking, she had responded in a light-hearted manner. Meanwhile, in the four weeks before he died, he was continuously playing a song about leaving that the family had not noticed him playing before. Mentioning to another friend that he wanted to be buried with a certain chain, could, looking back, be interpreted as another sign; however, people can discuss such matters casually, without any deeper meaning underlying what they are saying.

Darren's decision to take his own life was completely unexpected and apparently out of character. 'When you carry a child for nine months, you know what time they get up, you know what they eat, you know when something's wrong – but there was no indication with Darren.' His mother realises that there was a lot more going on under the surface than she realised and though she was incredibly close to her young son, he didn't tell her everything. There were things in Darren's life that weren't perfect. However, his happy-go-lucky attitude always gave the impression that there was nothing he was unable to cope with. His mother now believes that it was a combination of factors that resulted in the teenager feeling that the only way out was to take his own life.

Although a true leader and immensely popular in school, Darren was a target for bullies outside. There was rivalry among youths from different estates in the area where Darren lived and youths from one estate were not allowed to enter the other. Taught by his mother that it took a real man to walk away from a fight, Maureen believes Darren may have been an easy target for bullies. The attack in which his hand was injured had happened six weeks earlier. He had gone over to a takeaway and was passing through the rival estate with two friends, when they were jumped on by a much bigger group of youths. His mother says that on that occasion Darren fought back – for the first time ever, because he had to. 'He had been bullied by local thugs previously. They would take his money, his mobile phone and punch him for their entertainment. He'd often come home black and blue.'

Still, Darren had always seemed to put a brave face on it. His mother feels other circumstances combined with the bullying to create a sense of hopelessness. Darren was also in a band. He was always auditioning and on the lookout for opportunities. He had had some successes but he was impatient for things to take off there and then. Though he was only 16, he may have been feeling hopeless about his music career – that it wasn't going right and would not work out. He had also told his mother that he wanted to leave school.

Maureen believes that all the little things became magnified in Darren's mind, even silly quarrels with his brothers about clothes, eventually becoming too much and, instead of looking for help, the 16-year-old decided for himself that the future was hopeless and ended it all. 'The brothers would have the usual fights and arguments about clothes. There were occasions when I would get in between the boys to keep them apart and tell them to go into their rooms. Five minutes later, they seemed to have forgotten about it. It was all "Bro, can I borrow that hair Dax, Bro?"'

The shock of Darren's death has convinced Maureen that young people face a lot of difficulties and issues that may seem unimportant to adults, that they may even dismiss, but which can seem hugely significant in the mind of a teenager. She has learned that although herself and Darren could not have been closer, family can sometimes be too close to talk to about certain things.

Maureen is determined that no other mother should suffer the trauma that she has suffered and will continue to suffer for the rest of her life. She believes one of the most important factors in combating youth suicide is to give young people someone they can talk to, someone they are comfortable talking to, who is not as close as family, but who they know they can trust. She also wants young people to realise that suicide is final, forever – that there's no coming back.

Darren's body was brought to the family house and Maureen called on any of Darren's friends who wanted to, to come up to the house and see him laid out. 'I knew he was very well respected and looked up to. I wanted them to see that there was no coming back from suicide. Seeing is believing. I wanted them to see that Darren was not getting back up; he wasn't going to tell one of his jokes, that when you die by suicide you ground yourself for life.'

It's not just the individual who takes their life who is grounded. 'We, the family, are grounded too. We are the living dead.' Maureen knows her son would never have willingly put his family through this horror, which they will never get over, and she thinks it is vital that others understand that these are the real effects of suicide. A suicidal person may never consider the agonising aftermath that they will leave in their wake – often, they may feel that the people they love are better off without them, which couldn't be further from the truth. 'All the teenagers who have come to see me say that, since Darren's death, they have realised how much their families mean to them.'

For the rest of their lives, Maureen and her family will have only photographs of Darran. 'I will be lighting candles for the rest of my life. I've the rest of my life of Darren not getting off the school bus. Sometimes I cry buckets over Darren.' Every time Maureen sees teenagers pass by The Square, where Darren used to hang out, she is very conscious that Darren is no longer one of them. 'I still cook enough for five people.' Maureen will ask *Why?* for the rest of her life. 'Darren is the first thing you think of every morning and the last thing every night. I think of him constantly. Sometimes I feel guilty if I stop thinking about him for a second. I'm terrified I'll forget my son. When I pass his friends and they wave at me, I know he's not there, yet I still look for him in the crowd. Sometimes I see young boys who look exactly like Darren and once, though I knew it couldn't be my son, I still followed one boy around.' Every night, Maureen sleeps with the jumper her son was wearing on the day he died, clinging on to the final memories of her son. When she looks out the window on a sunny day and sees other young people passing by, she can't help but ask: 'Why isn't my son there?'

She now just takes each day as it comes. Some days she can't even get out of bed and she has sudden moments of realisation, when she's talking about Darren's death, that it is actually her son she is talking about. 'It's horrible when you're sitting there at ten past four and see the boys getting off the school bus. Some have haircuts like Darren and my stomach does a flip. I think about him constantly.'

Darren's brothers, 24-year-old Alan and 22-year-old Anthony are devastated. 'Part of all of us died with Darren,' and there is very little Maureen can do to ease her sons' pain. 'When they are children and they hurt themselves, you can kiss their knee better. This can never be kissed better.' The boys don't want to go for counselling, telling their mother that they'll deal with it in their own way. They don't like talking about Darren's death.

The idea for Teen-Line came to Maureen following conversations with Darren's teenage friends after he died. Maureen had always thought that she had nothing to worry about with Darren, and his suicide made her realise that a lot goes on in young people's minds that parents often don't realise. A group of about 15 teenagers, boys and girls, came over to see Maureen one day and she asked them what they would do if they needed someone to talk to. Would they ring Childline? Childline was viewed as a service for young children, while many thought the Samaritans were priests who wore frocks and none of them had even heard of Aware. The teenagers also told her that all of them had thought about suicide at some stage.

Maureen realised there was no specific service in place for teenagers who needed to talk and she asked them if there was a Teen-Line, whether they would feel comfortable calling if they had a problem or needed to talk to someone. The girls all said they would, while the boys said they didn't know. 'They were very open and honest. A teacher who works as a counsellor in schools is not enough. It's hard enough for a teenager to trust an adult and then have that same person teach them in class – especially if you've been crying.'

'Teenagers are told to dismiss little things and they can feel their opinion is undervalued.' Maureen says that, for example, teenagers' complaints about height and appearance can be perceived as trivial, although for the teenager they may be of massive importance.

'If awareness is not brought into schools, we'll lose more young people. All schools should have a qualified, paid counsellor that young people can talk to, as a bare minimum.' Maureen is anxious that positive mental health is actively promoted in schools and that young people are given the opportunity to discuss their problems in the educational environment. She feels the stigma surrounding the difficulties young people may experience needs to be removed. Teen-Line is a step towards removing the stigma and giving young people an opportunity to share their problems with someone who will listen to them. Maureen spoke to the Samaritans about providing a service specifically tailored to teenagers' needs, but funding was a problem. The Samaritans are now going to train volunteers for Teen-Line and fundraising is underway.

Teen-Line is now a registered charity and the service, which is set to kick off in mid-2006, will initially run from 8pm on a Friday until 8pm the following Monday. The service is provided by volunteers – counsellors and ordinary people 'with a good heart'. They have got premises and are working continuously to raise funds to keep the service up and running, with the long-term aim of establishing a location where teenagers are welcome to drop in. 'Teenagers have taught me so much. They are so honest and open; they know when you are really listening to them and they won't lie to you because they respect you for listening.'

'Teenagers don't want to die, but some of them can't cope living with the way our society is today. They think suicide might relieve the pain that's in their heads.' Maureen thinks that the pressures of modern society are particularly challenging for teenagers and believes that Ireland's economic success, though beneficial in certain areas, has not led to any improvement in the provision of leisure facilities for young people. 'I see all these high-rise buildings but there are very few facilities out there for teenagers – where can they go? There are bowling alleys, cinemas, but it's all very expensive. Where are they to get the money from?' Indeed, many of the organisations I interviewed for this book cite the establishment of a youth centre, where young people can go in their free time, as top of their list of objectives.

Maureen's observations reflect the diversity and complexity of the myriad issues that have an influence on the psychological well-being of teenagers and, indeed, human beings in general. While different people face different challenges throughout life, the factors that can lead an individual to feel low, frightened or in extreme cases, suicidal are innumerable and multifaceted. Examples of causes include inherent psychological illness, concerns about the future, minor disagreements with family members, inadequate social conditions, a lack of facilities, money worries, having nobody to share their problems with and a general lack of awareness and understanding in society. These are just a drop in the ocean in terms of the influences that affect mental health and they can all add up and become magnified. Indeed, as Dan Neville TD notes in his 2004 book, *Suicide Awareness*, the National Task Force on Suicide (published in 1998) outlined a list of 86 areas where interventions should be made to reduce the suicide levels.

Even bullies may not grasp the seriousness of the consequences that their actions can have. After Darren's death, Maureen went over to the area where the groups of youths involved in the inter-estate rivalry congregated. She went over to a group of young people and asked them whether they knew who she was. When they shook their heads, she told them she was Darren Bolger's mother and recognition crossed their faces. Maureen made it clear that she hadn't come to accuse them, but asked them to tell the perpetrators of the attacks on her son to put an end to the senseless fighting so that other young people would not be traumatised. Apart from the odd cheeky individual, the group showed respect to Maureen, with one even calling after her, 'Fair play, Mrs Bolger', and for a while a truce did appear to have been called.

While bullying is a factor in some suicides, no one can be certain that Darren's experience of bullying was responsible for his death by suicide. There is no clear-cut evidence of a direct link between bullying and suicide; however, research has indicated that 15 to 20 per cent of all deaths by suicide may be caused by bullying. Suicide is hugely complex and there is general consensus among those who have done extensive research into the area that suicides are caused by a range of complex burdens on the suicidal person. The next chapter looks at the connection between suicide and bullying.

Teen-Line's freephone number will be launched in mid-2006. In the meantime, if you need someone to talk to, do not hesitate to contact Maureen (085 741 6019) or Eithne (085 741 7934) at any time.

Suicide and Bullying

Although figures for suicide as a direct result of bullying are not available for Ireland, it has been estimated that up to 12 children die by suicide in the UK each year as a direct result of being bullied. Many more suicides, however, are believed to be associated with bullying. In 1999, an eight-year-old girl in the UK took her life after she said she was being bullied, highlighting how serious an effect bullying can have on very young people. Still, cases such as these are the exception to the rule.

According to Andrew Mellors, manager of the anti-bullying network at the University of Edinburgh, if we accept the widely used figure of 12 children a year in the UK dying by suicide that has been motivated by bullying (and it is impossible to prove), a school would have a 1 in 3,000 chance of a suicide occurring as a direct result of bullying in any one year (2002 IAS Conference on Bullying and Suicide in Schools). He points out that although this makes the likelihood of an actual suicide occurring in a school minimal, bullying can result in many more children contemplating suicide, which makes them likely to carry permanent psychological and emotional scars. Of considerable concern are studies that show that victims of bullying are significantly more likely to have attempted suicide.

Children who are repeatedly bullied report higher levels of thoughts about suicide or suicide ideation than other students. In studies, children who were bullied most often were much more inclined to generally associate school with a feeling of unhappiness than those who weren't. Particularly worrying are the results from a study of suicidal ideation in a sample of over 800 Australian secondary school children: those children (approximately 15 per cent) who were victims of bullying were much more prone to suicidal ideation than others. Children who are bullied in school also report feeling depressed after suffering bullying. Depression is strongly associated with suicide, so even if the bullying is not a direct cause of an individual taking their life, bullying is one of the many factors that can affect and contribute to suicidal ideation in an individual at the time of being bullied, or indeed in later life. Speaking at the 2002 IAS conference, Dr Mona O'Moore warned that bullies themselves do not escape unscathed either: 'Research has shown that children who bully are also at risk of depression and suicide ideation, thoughts of suicide being more severe than in victims.'

On 16 April 1998, *The Irish Times* reported the case of a student at UCG who took his life after suffering years of bullying at school. Reporting on the inquest, *The Irish Times* stated: 'The 20-year-old UCG student was subjected to years of physical, verbal, and racial abuse in a school in a west of Ireland town.'

The fact that a child or young person is being bullied and, in turn, becomes depressed and contemplates suicide could point to other underlying causes and there is the argument that a child's family background, as well as other circumstances in their lives, could contribute to them becoming a victim of bullying in the first place. As there are numerous factors in a person's life that can affect their level of mental health, bullying can not stand alone as a cause of suicide. Indeed, Dr John Connolly points out that, 'Often we tend to see the final circumstances as a cause of the suicide and this is too simplistic. After detailed examination of the circumstances, [...] it is often difficult to say if bullying was the only, or main cause of the tragedy. Other factors are usually involved.'

Professor Ken Rigby warned that while bad parenting is often cited as a factor contributing to a child being bullied at school, this explanation can often be mistaken. Speaking at the 2002 IAS Conference on Bullying, Prof. Rigby said that being badly treated by one's parents does not generally make one a victim at school: 'Of course, as we know, parents are sometimes accountable for the deep unhappiness of their children. However, to trace a child's unhappiness or psychopathology to parental miscare can often be mistaken.'

Still, there is a definite connection between suicide and bullying and the effects of bullying are likely to have a lasting detrimental effect on the present and future mental health of a schoolchild. How much bullying at school contributes to future mental health problems associated with suicide may also be significant according to Dr John Connolly.

He also points out that dropping out of the educational system is associated with suicide and suicidal behaviour. He stresses the importance of promoting good mental health 'and where better to do this than in our schools?'

Speaking at the 2002 Conference on Bullying and Suicide in Schools, a young lady, Elaine Doyle, told of her personal traumatic experience of bullying in secondary school, which led her to think about ending it all on numerous occasions. Elaine read from a piece of writing that she had written a few weeks after she changed school, describing the traumatic effects the experience of bullying was having on her psychological and emotional well-being: 'Words could not possibly express the feelings you suffer … isolation … rejection … insecurity … depression […]. It feels like the whole world is pressing down on you and there is no escape.'

Elaine was bullied in her senior years of secondary school. She didn't tell her parents for months. In hindsight, she believes the motivation for not telling them was a mixture of feeling ashamed, not wanting to admit it and not fully understanding what was happening.

It all began in her Leaving Certificate year. Elaine was handed back a Physics exam for which she had studied very hard. The teacher made a big deal that just one person in the class had got 100 per cent in the exam – that person was Elaine. Elaine was over the moon that her hard work had paid off, but that was when the bullying started and her life took a drastic turn for the worse.

People began to write horrible things about her in the school bathrooms, on desks, on her locker and in notes that were being passed around. Outside school in the town, the bullying continued. For some reason, people were calling her Barbie and groups would sing the song 'Barbie Girl' in the town. She was also threatened outside school and, on one occasion, she was pinned up against the wall by a group of girls and a fist was held up to her.

She said life was unbearable and she changed school. Though she made friends at her new school, the bullying continued outside. Elaine's whole life had become miserable and on a weekend away in Clifden with her family, she eventually broke down and told her parents. She recalls how, that weekend, she was watching the rest of her family having great fun in the swimming-pool and she just couldn't join them. 'I just didn't want to be around anyone ... I stood watching them with tears in my eyes ... I hated seeing them so happy and I just couldn't force myself to even smile.'

Elaine felt so alone, so afraid, as if she was trapped in a nightmare. 'I just couldn't get out of it. I didn't feel safe anywhere, not even at home because no matter where I was, there was so much going on in my head, I could never escape the torture.' Her self-esteem and confidence were destroyed and she became extremely paranoid and pessimistic.

Once her parents realised what was going on, they did everything in their power to help her, but, as Elaine points out, parents do not receive training on how to deal with their child if they are being bullied and though some things they did for Elaine were helpful, others were not so helpful. It was a very difficult time for Elaine and her family. She says that she became the daughter and sister from hell, locking herself in her room, screaming at them and running away from the house. She started drinking very heavily at weekends.

Elaine also thought of taking her life on numerous occasions. 'I reached the stage where I believed I was the problem and that everyone would be better off if I was gone. I also felt that nobody would notice me gone or even miss me ... it seemed like the only solution to all of my problems ...'

Though Elaine is a much stronger person now, the experience has left some scars. 'Even now, I find it very difficult to trust people, which has affected many of my relationships with people. In particular, it takes me a long time to trust girls ... I get to a certain stage, and then the barrier goes up.' Elaine says she is one of the lucky ones as she has come through the traumatic experience and she wonders, 'How many more lives have to be destroyed and lost before the government takes this issue seriously?'

Consultant psychiatrist with the North Eastern Health Board (NEHB), Dr Maria Lawlor, who initiated the NEHB's 'Cool School' anti-bullying programme for second-level schools, told the 2002 Conference on Bullying and Suicide in Schools that findings in the North Eastern region of Ireland reveal that 15 per cent of young people in second-level schools are victims of bullying. Dr Lawlor spoke of an established link between bullying and depression. Research carried out in the NEHB region showed that many victims of bullying felt depressed and that one in five victims reported feeling suicidal – a frightening 21 per cent of victims. Those who experienced psychological bullying and social exclusion were most distressed, which Dr Lawlor says is noteworthy as the impact of psychological bullying is not commonly recognised in society: many people perceive bullying as being predominantly physical in nature.

Young people are sometimes referred to Accident and Emergency departments with the physical effects of bullying and, with regard to adolescents, a number of those referred with parasuicidal and self-harm behaviour have had experiences of bullying in school. The effects of bullying on schoolchildren are many and can contribute to eating disorders and depression in very young children.

The 'Cool School' programme aims to support schools in developing effective strategies to prevent and combat bullying behaviour and to reduce the extent and effects of bullying. The programme also organises in-service training for teachers and runs therapeutic groups for victims of bullying, as well as providing five lesson plans as part of the Student Curriculum for all students.

Dr Lawlor feels that preventing one of the reasons why young people feel suicidal is likely to help prevent suicides and she says, 'an effective anti-bullying programme in schools is one essential facet of an adolescent suicide prevention strategy'. The NEHB 'Cool School' anti-bullying programme's book is entitled *Bullying in Secondary School: What Parents Need to Know.*

The 2002 seminar emphasised the need to affirm the self-esteem and self-worth of each individual and the need to treat each individual with respect and dignity.

While the Irish Association of Suicidology's National Conference in 2002 focused on bullying and suicide in schools, bullying and its related effects stretch across all facets of society, including the home and workplace.

Speaking at the 2002 IAS conference, Bullying and Suicide in Schools, Dr Mona O'Moore referred to the National Survey of Workplace Bullying which she conducted through the Anti-Bullying Centre at Trinity College in 2001: 'We learned that one in twenty adults reported that they had suicidal thoughts [...] For those victims who had decided on a course of legal action, one half had considered suicide as a real option.' Bullying in the workplace can take many forms, according to Rev. Dr Tony Byrne. He lists examples of bullying at work to include reducing people's workloads, not inviting them to meetings, moving their desks to peripheral areas of offices, belittling their roles through jokes or comments, excluding them from decisions and expecting them to come to work every day with nothing to do. People need to become acutely aware of bullying before they can end it, according to Rev. Dr Tony Byrne.

Although exact figures are not available for the incidence of suicide as a direct result of bullying in Ireland, reseachers estimate that 15–20 per cent of all suicides are caused by bullying. Still, as Rev. Dr Tony Byrne points out in the book, *Bullying in the Workplace, Home and School*, it is very difficult to pinpoint one single cause of suicide. 'Suicidologists believe that suicides are caused by cumulative burdens on the suicidal person.' No matter how much bullying may appear to be to blame in any particular case of suicide, no one can ever say for sure that it is the cause. In the section of the book that deals with bullying in the home, Sr Kathleen Maguire points out that in some extreme cases of domestic bullying, adolescents consider the option of suicide. 'They usually do not tell their parents about their suicidal intentions, but sometimes tell their peers.'

Bullying, whether it is in the workplace, home or school, has numerous negative psychological effects. It has been described as a psychological terror and though it is impossible to say that there is a direct link between bullying and suicide, there is no doubt that bullying is a factor in some suicides, according to Dr Brendan Byrne, who answers questions in the section of the book on bullying in school. 'Severe bullying that has gone on for a long period may lead to feelings of anger and sadness, which may in turn lead to suicidal ideation. It is certain that bullying leads to feelings of humiliation and a lowering of self-worth. In these circumstances, it is more likely that a person will consider suicide.'

An information pack that includes a comprehensive reading list in a booklet entitled *School Bullying: Key Facts* can be ordered free of charge from the Anti-Bullying Centre (ABC) at 01 608 2573/608 3488 or lmcguire@tcd.ie.

If you or someone you know is being bullied and you are looking for information and support, contact the 24-hour anti-bullying hotline on the following numbers:

Daytime (9am–8pm): 0502 61666

Night-time (8pm–9am): 00502 10598

If you would like a copy of the information pack *Let's Talk Bullying*, call the daytime number above.

Jean Casey: The Story of a Pregnant Young Mother Losing her Husband

A professional IACP (Irish Association for Counselling and Psychotherapy) counsellor who specializes in the suicide and homicide bereaved, Jean Casey is an individual very familiar with the subject of suicide, from both a professional and personal point of view. Her academic career in counselling began after her husband died by suicide on the 13 August 1977. Jean was only 27. Padraic and Jean had three small daughters – Catherine who was six, Eileen who was five and Ruth who was three. Jean was also three months' pregnant – her daughter Una was born six months later. Padraic took his life in 1977, when suicide was still a crime in Ireland and hence a very taboo subject. Enveloped in a culture of silence, there was little support in Ireland for people like Jean, who were left in a terrible state of shock and bereavement.

At the time of his death, Jean did not suspect for a moment that her husband could ever be in so much pain that he would consider such a desperate and final act. The family had few worries, financial or otherwise: Padraic's job was going well and the children were doing great. They had even moved into their second house off Griffith Avenue in Dublin, which was bigger and nicer than the first.

Armed with the wisdom of hindsight, Jean now understands that her husband may have been depressed about a work issue that he had spoken about. Padraic was the manager of a pub and things had been going wrong. There was an issue over money being taken and stock going missing and, as the manager, he felt responsible and also feared that the owner may have thought it was he who was taking it. Jean feels he was struggling with that and that that resulted in him becoming very depressed, though she didn't realise it back then. 'I didn't know what depression was at the time. He became withdrawn, stopped eating and was quiet and sad. He didn't know how to solve it.' Jean recalls noticing this in the two weeks before he died, but never did she even imagine that things were so bad that he would consider suicide. The two had married when Jean was just 20 and he was 22. She really believed that she knew him very well and the idea that a difficulty in his life would result in his suicide was alien to her.

The Saturday that Padraic died, he had taken the car out to do some shopping earlier that day, as Jean was feeling unwell due to her pregnancy. On his way to the shops, Padraic was involved in a collision with a bus. He was taken to hospital but was later discharged, as he had no serious injuries. He came home that evening and went straight to bed. The only physical sign of the accident was a cut on his foot, but he was in deep shock. Realising this, Jean called the family doctor and asked him to come and see Padraic. The doctor confirmed that Padraic was indeed suffering from shock and gave him some sleeping tablets. Leaving him to get some sleep, Jean put her youngest daughter to bed and decided to go and do the shopping that Padraic had originally gone out to do before his accident. She left with her two other daughters at about eight o'clock, returning home roughly an hour later. She arrived back to find their bedroom door locked.

Thinking he must have taken the sleeping tablets, but very confused as to why he would lock the door (something he had never done before), Jean put the other children to bed and then tried to waken him and get the door open. When there was no response, Jean was very concerned and knew she would need help getting the door open, so she called the local Gardaí. Two Gardaí came out to the house and Jean brought them upstairs to the locked bedroom. They managed to break the lock and Jean followed the first Garda into the bedroom. Her husband was lying dead on the floor. A member of a gun club, Padraic had shot himself in the head with his rifle. He was only 29 years old.

Realising what had happened, the Gardaí immediately rushed her out of the bedroom, but not before she had witnessed the horrific sight of her husband, dead by his own hand. They had always had the rifle in the bedroom, but it had never even been loaded. Shooting was a hobby for Padraic, but Jean had never in her life imagined for a moment that Padraic would use his rifle on himself. The sight of Padraic's body was so horrendous that, following the discovery, one of the Gardaí had to rush into the bathroom to be sick. The other Garda went down to the kitchen with Jean and asked her if she had known that her husband had a firearm. She told him that shooting was Padraic's hobby. Fortunately, the children slept through all of the commotion. Although the youngest girl was in the house when Padraic took his life, she would have heard nothing as he had the silencer on. At that point, Jean received a phone call from her sister who lived in Drogheda and she told her what had just happened. Her sister told their parents and then she immediately came over to Jean's house. Then, more Gardaí arrived and Jean, already traumatised, received another big shock that very evening.

More Gardaí had arrived because a murder investigation had been launched – and Jean was the prime suspect. They started to question Jean: 'I knew I was a suspect. It was horrible.' Only 27 years of age, three months' pregnant, under the severe shock of having just lost her husband to suicide, she was now under suspicion of murder. Fortunately, the Gardaí found the suicide note shortly after they had begun questioning her and she was no longer under investigation.

The children slept soundly through the night and the next day Jean knew she would have to tell them that their father was dead; she decided at the time not to tell them that he had died by suicide and instead said that their daddy had died during the night as a result of the car accident. In hindsight, she believes she should have told them the full truth at the time. In the days that followed his death, Jean felt completely numb. She was shocked and filled with fear at the thought of facing the future alone, without her husband of seven years: 'I was three months' pregnant and fearful for the future. How would I rear the children? I didn't have a clue about finances. How would I survive?' Also running through her mind was the unanswerable *Why?* 'Why, why did he do this? Why did it happen? I thought we had a good marriage. I just couldn't understand it.'

In the aftermath of his death, Jean started going over the previous year of Padraic's life and looking at his childhood, analysing his whole life, searching for some clue to try and figure out what could possibly have caused her husband to take such drastic action. 'I still don't know the *Why*. I have to accept there's no real answer to the *Why?* question. You can never know the deep recesses of a person's mind. I thought I knew him really well.'

Looking back over the period before he died, Jean did remember something Padraic had said two weeks before his suicide, which could have indicated what he was planning, but again many idle comments can be made that don't necessarily mean anything. He had said to Jean, 'If anything happens to me, my family and your family will look after you.' Jean didn't think anything of it. Another thing that she felt could have been a sign was the fact that, around the time he died, he had been reading a book that had described a suicide in graphic detail around the time he died. He was into popular horror books anyway, but millions of people are and his reading material was certainly not a cause for concern.

Padraic was a very ambitious man. He had wanted to own his own pub eventually and was working his way up. He had started as a bar man and had become manager of a bigger pub. 'He used to say he'd have his own pub at 30, at 40 he'd have a hotel and by the age of 50 he'd have a chain. He was dedicated and very ambitious at work.' Any time he had off he would spend with his family. 'We had lots of friends and would go out a lot together.' Jean didn't think there was any problem in their marriage. 'He loved the girls. We were very happy.'

As Jean mulled over the various incidents in his life that could have played some role in Padraic's suicide, she remembered that his 14-year-old sister had died when Padraic was only 13 years old. She feels that this could have been a factor that interacted with other circumstances in his later years, affecting his state of mind. 'She had cancer and the family were nursing her at home. She died in Padraic's arms when he was only 13. It was pretty awful for him.' Padraic had also mentioned events in school to her, something regarding physical abuse, but she wasn't sure of the details. But all of these elements still did not provide an answer and Jean, to this very day, still does not know why the man she loved and the father of her children took his life and left them behind. The hastily scribbled suicide note found in the couple's bedroom gave no clue either, with the simple text: 'I'm sorry, Darling Jean. I've always loved you. Pray for me.'

The inquest took place three months after Padraic's death. Jean's brother and her husband's brother came with her. Though Jean was happy with how the inquest was handled, she still found the experience 'pretty awful', with all the details of her husband's death being brought up again. She had to get up in the witness stand in public. 'It was harrowing.' Jean is now campaigning to change the courtroom format in the case of suicides. She feels inquests should be held in private and should not be open to the public. Indeed, this is an issue that many people who have lost loved ones to suicide feel very strongly about and some coroners have taken moves to ensure that suicide inquests are held with just the family and necessary official figures present. (See Chapter 13 – Improving the Inquest Process.) Jean had to sit through the minute details of six other suicides before the details of Padraic's came up. 'It was pretty gruesome. I felt the wait was awful. I didn't want to listen to anyone else's.'

Jean had spent the past nine years of her life with her husband, married for seven of them. 'I knew him since he was 20.' She was now faced with the daunting task of raising four children all alone, with no partner to talk to. Una, who was born six months after Padraic's death, would never know her father. Jean waited until each one of the girls was 12 years of age before telling them that their dad had died by suicide. In hindsight, with her experience both personally and professionally, she recommends telling children straight away. By not telling the children that it was suicide immediately, she was faced with the burden and pressure of keeping it a constant secret. The children grew up thinking that their father had died as the result of a car crash.

'Catherine was the first to be told about the suicide when she turned 12. She was shocked and wanted to share it with others, but I didn't want others to know. She asked me could she tell her best friend and I said she could.' But, when Catherine told her best friend, she found out that she already knew; her parents had told her. 'She was hurt and devastated that her friend knew and she didn't.'

The following year, her second daughter, Eileen, was told. 'She took it differently. Eileen wanted to know the gory details. She adjusted very well.' The following year, the third daughter was told. 'It was easier telling the second and third daughters as they could talk to the girls who had already been told about it.' Jean's third daughter, Ruth, didn't believe it could be just because of the job. She thought there had to be something more to it and she started searching for reasons. 'She got me into doing that as well.' Una, who was born after her father died, took it the worst as she felt her dad didn't want her coming.

Unfortunately, there was very little support available for either Jean or the children. In 1977, work in the area of suicide bereavement was nowhere near where it is today. 'No-one ever suggested I should go for counselling.' Suicide was a serious taboo subject and, though the one thing Jean probably needed most was to talk about it, everyone tried to avoid the subject: 'People would tell me not to talk about it, not to upset myself. I got to the stage where I couldn't even mention his name then, but all I wanted to do was talk about it.' In a practical sense, everyone was very good to her, especially both Padraic's and her own family and neighbours, but Jean needed to talk, 'I had a hunger to meet someone else who had been bereaved by suicide.'

It was seven long years before Jean eventually heard about a counselling centre in Dublin. 'I went for counselling and I have never looked back since.' Jean even decided that she wanted to become a counsellor herself. 'I realised that people needed to talk about it, analyse and dissect what happened, which is what I did until I couldn't do it anymore. That's what people need to do. They need to go for counselling and then go into a group. That's where you can identify with other people.'

In an environment where suicide was illegal and people were anxious to avoid any mention of the word, Jean realised that denial would help no-one. 'I made a point of letting everyone know he died by suicide. People would say, "Don't say that word," but it helped me to be totally honest and out of denial. When people are in denial, they don't recover well.'

Twenty-eight years have now passed since Padraic died so tragically and the children are now grown up and married. 'They all seem to be doing fine.' Jean says, 'Inevitably, their father's death by suicide affects them and always will.'

As a direct result of her own personal experience with suicide, Jean has studied and read everything she could find about the psychological determinants of suicide and it has been a professional interest for more than 15 years.

Jean now operates as a counsellor from her practice in Co. Louth. She specialises in the treatment of the suicide and homicide bereaved and also works as a supervisor for other counsellors as well. Jean is a founding member of Console, the Bereaved by Suicide Foundation, based in Dublin. She was instrumental in starting a Console group in Galway as well and is heavily involved in training others throughout the country to become counsellors.

Though the tragedy of her husband's suicide back in 1977 will never leave Jean, her personal story is evidence of the fact that life does go on. As part of the suicide bereavement workshops she organises, she reminds people that though they must know they will never be the same again, you can survive and even go beyond surviving. The first of her 25 suggestions for survivors in an April 2005 course book for a Suicide Bereavement Workshop is 'Know you can survive. You may not think so, but you can.' Jean also advises those bereaved by suicide to struggle with the *Why?* it happened 'until you no longer need to know why or until you are satisfied with partial answers'.

Dealing with Suicide: A Garda's Perspective

Every suicide has a tremendous effect on a huge number of family and friends – experts estimate that, on average, six people will be seriously affected by each suicide and a huge number of others will be affected to a lesser extent. Beyond immediate family and friends, however, suicide also takes its toll on members of the wider community, including nurses, doctors, parish priests and the Gardaí. Interestingly, of these groups, doctors, nurses and the Gardaí all have high suicide rates in Ireland.

Retired Garda, Michael Egan, recalls the first time he was called to the scene of a suicide – he was just 26 years of age. 'It was a Saturday night and I was on duty. We received a call to say a body had been sighted floating in the water.' He recalls the intense fear he experienced on arriving at the scene. 'Seeing the body terrified me. I knew I would have to ensure everything was right for the subsequent inquest and I was terrified I would be asked to physically handle the body. I knew I wouldn't have been able for it.' At that time, there was no protective clothing or gloves provided for such incidents. Finding the body of someone who has died by suicide will have a harrowing effect on any human being, and it was certainly a shock to the system for young Michael, but as he would discover very soon afterwards, it was a shock that would be repeated many times during his career.

Wearing a uniform does not, unfortunately, lessen the emotional strain that a person who has to attend the scene of a suicide will experience. The huge level of responsibility borne by a Garda in these circumstances only serves to increase the pressure on them. In a matter of minutes, if not seconds, Gardaí must make a call on whether the death is suicide or not. The urgency with which this decision must be made and the repercussions it will have cannot be overstated. In the presence of distraught family members, the Garda relies on his/her professional training and experience to decide if it was, indeed, suicide or if there is sufficient doubt to warrant investigating further; that would involve cordoning the area off, preserving the scene, calling the coroner and, perhaps, causing further distress and confusion for the person's family.

Making the call on whether the person has died by their own hand or somebody else's, i.e. whether it's a suicide or a homicide, is one of the most difficult and delicate situations a Garda can find himself/herself in. It is not unknown for the Gardaí to suspect foul play initially, only to realise later that the injuries were self-inflicted. This is very traumatic for the Garda, who must then re-visit the family and tell them of the mistake, explaining that not only is their loved one dead, but they actually chose to take their own life. In such an eventuality, no matter how difficult the prospect is, the Garda needs to give the family the news straight away, as the sooner they are told exactly what happened, the sooner their healing can commence. If the death appears to be a suicide, the first question the Garda must consider is the method of death and whether or not it is physically possible for a person to take their life in that way without assistance.

Today, Garda Egan recalls the fear and anxiety that marked that first suicide he came across. 'What was running through my mind was that I had to do it all right, from A–Z.' Having satisfied himself that this was indeed a suicide, his next big concern was how to identify the body. The other worry preying on his mind was the task of notifying the person's family, after which, he would have to accompany a family member to the morgue to carry out a formal identification. Then, the responsibility for formally identifying the body to the pathologist would rest with him.

Less than 12 hours after attending that first suicide, Garda Michael Egan was called to the river to attend to another suicide by drowning. People sometimes forget that Gardaí are human too. Although senior members of the force may have a lot more experience in dealing with matters such as these, it is a huge shock to the system for a younger member of the force.

In the days and weeks that followed the two suicides, Michael couldn't sleep. He was fearful about what would happen at the subsequent inquests. 'A Garda has to go and view the body, handle the body and deal with their own feelings. You can't go home and talk about these things to your young wife. Although the other Gardaí were helpful and supportive, Michael points out that, at the end of the day, you have to deal with your own fears on your own. Michael's particular fear was of touching dead bodies, which made dealing with these cases all the more frightening for him.

He eventually got over his fear of touching corpses, thanks to the help of a young nurse who explained to him that it felt just like touching marble. Still, nothing can prepare anyone, a Garda or otherwise, for the particularly horrific circumstances surrounding suicide and, as time went on, Michael would see many. Over his career, he was called to the scenes of a total of 12 suicides. 'Apart from drownings, the shootings and hangings are particularly horrific. Body parts are literally everywhere after a shooting. If a long period of time has passed between the death and the discovery of the body, the body can be in an awful state and very difficult to identify.'

Michael says it is particularly awful when a person throws themselves under a train. A huge number of people are affected by the scene – it is a shock for the passengers on the train and it is particularly devastating for the driver, who, for about two miles, has no way of stopping the train and has to witness the death. It is horrible for anyone to learn that a family member has died in this manner and the Gardaí make every effort to minimise the family's anguish. One of the ways they do this is by literally picking up body pieces that are scattered along the tracks.

Michael recalls the first suicide post-mortem he attended and the fear it aroused in him. It is commonly acknowledged that it is beneficial to talk about what's going on at times like these. However, it is also widely acknowledged that men are not particularly good at discussing their emotions, something that was highlighted for Michael by the reaction of one of his colleagues on the day of the post-mortem. Micheal learned later that this colleague just didn't know how to cope with Michael's obvious distress and, although he knew that he was in need of support, he was afraid that Michael would cry.

'Women can deal with crying, but men cannot deal with another man crying.' Michael feels there should be a support procedure in place for members of the force. He said it could make a significant and positive difference, 'even if your senior were to say, "You were out on an incident, how are you feeling?", rather than "You were out on an incident, where's the report?".' With an approximate four-to-one ratio of male to female suicides in Ireland, it is inevitable that rates of Garda suicide will reflect the national trend, and being a typically male-dominated career, rates will be higher than in other professions. By the nature of the work the Gardaí carry out, they can find themselves taking home a complex range of issues and emotions that they then have to deal with alone. True to the profile of the typical Irish male, when something goes wrong, they often don't talk about it. Furthermore, Garda confidentiality prevents them from discussing the details of their work openly.

Garda Michael Egan has used his own experience as a young Garda dealing with suicide to devise a training programme for future generations of Gardaí. He wants to make it easier for both the bereaved families and the Garda dealing with the suicide. 'I started researching the issue in 1989, approaching the questions that face every Garda when dealing with a suicide, from how to break the bad news, to understanding what families expect from the Gardaí. I approached Mary Begley, a former suicide research officer with the Mid-Western Health Board.'

Mary and Michael decided they would approach people that they knew had been bereaved by suicide and find out what they would have liked from the Gardaí at the time. Based on his research, Garda Egan compiled a series of recommendations on how to break the bad news to a family following a suicide, and when he became a trainer at Templemore Garda Training College, student Gardaí were trained accordingly. Sharing his own experience of fear and superstition with his students, he explained that there's no need to be afraid and that it's good to discuss their fears with their sergeant. 'It is not as bad if you can talk about it.' Regarding breaking the bad news, Michael says, 'Breaking the bad news is very difficult. You have to try to be truthful and not cause any further pain. We learn from mistakes.'

Breaking the Bad News

The work carried out by Garda Egan to date is indicative of the huge effort that has been made in Ireland to ensure that the pain experienced by bereaved people is not added to by those who deal with them. Michael has discovered that pain can be minimised by paying attention to certain details and he highlights examples of how everyone, not just the Gardaí, can play a role in this. Michael stresses that breaking the bad news is very difficult. 'You have to try to be truthful and not cause any further pain. We learn from mistakes.'

It is of crucial importance to have the correct name and address when breaking the bad news, as any mistakes can cause considerable trauma to both the family who have lost someone and to other individuals who are mistakenly informed that they have lost someone to suicide. There have been cases of mistaken identity, especially in rural Ireland, where several families with the same name may live beside each other. 'Unless you know their nickname, there is the risk of calling to the wrong house.' After talking to bereaved families and learning of the experience of other Gardaí, Michael realised that it was essential to check and double-check that Gardaí are informing the correct family. When a family realises that they were not the first to know of their loved one's death, it causes considerable hurt and, indeed, anger. They need to process and take in the trauma of what has happened before they decide how and who to tell and if neighbours already know, this element of control over the situation has been taken away from them. 'When such a mistake is established by the Gardaí, though it is extremely difficult, they need to immediately find the correct family and break the news.'

It is also essential to state the relationship of the deceased person before breaking the news of what has happened. Father and son can sometimes share the same name and getting it wrong and having to correct the situation afterwards will add to the pain of the bereaved unecessarily.

As can be seen from the many personal stories in this book, families want the full details of their loved one's death. Learning of a loved one's death is always a tremendous shock and those left behind want to know what happened, how it happened, when, where and why. With suicide, the *Why?* can rarely be fully answered, but it is essential to provide the information that is available. Michael advises the Gardaí to ensure that they have all the relevant details regarding the death – where the body was found, who recovered it and the name of the doctor who certified death. Relatives will also want to know where the body is now – the church or the hospital – and how it got there. Was it taken in an ambulance or a hearse? They will want to know every detail surrounding the person's death.

For the sake of both the Garda and the bereaved person(s), it is strongly recommended that the Garda should be accompanied when delivering the bad news. Firstly, there is the practical consideration. A person who has just learned that their loved one has died is in need of initial support. 'Stay with them when you break the news. A million and one things can be bothering the person.' Michael recalls breaking the news of a death in the early stages of his career. 'I remember my sergeant once told me to break bad news to a family. I'll remember it to this very day, standing outside the gate, wondering what to say. It was a fatal accident. I had to go with common sense and natural compassion. I didn't know until years after that I should have stayed with her [the bereaved woman]. On your own, it can be very stressful.' One of the Gardaí may be needed to follow up on the practicalities of the death, for example, accompanying a family member to officially identify the body. In such an instance, with two Gardaí present, one can remain with other family members and offer them support.

Another simple reason for two Gardaí going is the fact that neighbours will be calling in and families will want to offer them something – a cup of tea, for example. If one of the Gardaí can go down to the shops and get a few things, it can make a big difference to the family – this is where a Garda is very much a part of the community. In practical terms, families can understandably be very angry when they are confronted with the tragic news and Gardaí can be very frightened calling to a house. Although uncommon, there is always the threat of physical violence as well.

The actual wording used when informing someone of the death of a loved one needs to be carefully chosen, especially when the death is by suicide. What do you say? Michael recommends that once the person has answered the door, and it is established that it's the correct house, the opening remarks should be 'Sorry, I've bad news for you,' and to say nothing further until the person responds. 'Let them choose where to break the bad news. The sooner they are told the better.'

Michael says it should never be blurted out that it was a suicide. He recommends not using the word 'suicide', suggesting instead 'Guards have finished their enquiries. They have ruled out foul play and it wasn't an accident.' He further stresses the importance of avoiding such words as 'committed', 'sin', 'investigation' and 'crime', saying 'investigation' can be replaced with 'inquiry'. All questions must be answered honestly and if the Garda is asked whether it was a suicide, the truth must be told.

The research Michael carried out with bereaved families revealed that, in the case of suicide, professionals rarely sympathised with the family. 'This heightened the stigma. When we asked why the Gardaí and others did not sympathise, they said they did not know what to do.' It is important to offer your sympathies once you have broken the bad news, as not to do so would increase any feelings of guilt or stigma that the family may be feeling.

Individuals bereaved by suicide have often posed the question of who should be informed of the death first. For example, at a conference on suicide in 2005, a man wondered why the Gardaí had not informed him of his brother's death before his mother, as he felt he would have been better able to break the news to her. Experience has shown, however, that if a Garda calls to a house and does not tell the person available what has happened because they feel it more appropriate to break the news to someone else, considerable pain and confusion can arise. This is especially relevant in the case of a very young person answering the door. I asked Michael what a Garda should do if they call to a house and a 15- or 16-year-old is the only person in the house. Michael says that there have been cases where Gardaí have held off breaking the news until an adult was home; however, this has created huge trauma for the young person. 'A young person's imagination could run wild ... it may be a sibling that has died, but they could be thinking that their parents are dead.' Michael advises that Gardaí stay with the young person and answer their questions openly and honestly, while they find out where the parents or guardians are. The young person will have to find out eventually and the best approach is to be honest.

While some people feel that the appearance of an officer in uniform at your front door can be very shocking, a lot of bereaved families have reported that the sight of the uniform often begins the grieving process.

As suicide was decriminalised in 1993 some people have questioned why the Gardaí continue to be involved at all. Garda Egan says that their role changes; they are acting as coroner's officers, compiling the information for the coroner's inquest. This raises another issue concerning deaths by suicide – if suicide is decriminalised, why does an inquest have to be held at all?

An inquest can take anything from a matter of weeks to 14 months, which can add to families' trauma. In the North of Ireland, it lies at the discretion of the coroner whether they want to hold an inquest, while in the Republic an inquest is mandatory. Michael believes that the system in the North should also be introduced into the Republic. While on some levels, the inquest can set a lot of matters straight, especially if neighbours are discussing the incident and confusing facts, he believes that changes should be introduced.

Above all, he feels that the inquest should not be held in a courtroom, rather, it should be held in a less intimidating setting – a feeling shared by many others who have been affected in some way by suicide.

There are also practical problems for the families waiting for the inquest to take place. If the person who died is a business person, no bills can be paid without the death certificate from the inquest. Although some coroners will issue a certificate of the fact of death to allow people to move on, this is not always accepted by financial institutions. Garda Egan feels the Coroners' Act of 1962 is way past its sell-by-date.

As a result of his contact with families bereaved by suicide, Michael was prompted to set up an organisation called Living Links. 'People were saying that it would be really helpful if there was an organisation that would call to the house when they lost someone to suicide, rather than them having to go to a support group and share their stories with others. Despite the fact that there are support groups there, people are travelling long, long distances in order to maintain anonymity.'

Living Links was set up in 2002 with the express aim of providing a listening support service. Typically, when a tragedy occurrs in a family, neighbours and friends constantly call in and the family tell the story over and over again. When it's a suicide, this is not as typical as people just don't know what to say. Through Living Links, volunteers will visit the family if they request it. Families can call the number of a central coordinator and a volunteer is then dispatched. Depending on what the family want, it can be just one visit, or as many as 20.

Living Links is now in place in North Tipperary, Limerick, Kerry, Meath and Galway and volunteers are being trained in Dublin and Wicklow. Organisations in other counties have been in touch with Michael Egan, expressing interest in setting up Living Links in their areas. Volunteers undergo an intensive training programme, which includes a session with a psychiatrist who gives a presentation on the nature of suicide, while the Samaritans train volunteers in listening skills and introduce practical exercises. The Gardaí also discuss their role and a person who has been bereaved shares their story.

Michael hopes to see a national Living Links eventually and would like to see the introduction of a system currently in operation in the Netherlands. 'When a suicide occurs in the Netherlands, the person's GP writes to the family to inform them of services available, a copy of the letter is also sent to the outreach services, so when an individual does seek help, they already know the details of the suicide and don't need to keep going through the details.'

In the first year of Living Links, 12 calls were received; in 2004, this went up to 72 and in the first half of 2005, there had already been 65 calls. All calls are strictly confidential.

Losing Two Brothers to Suicide

Losing one family member to suicide is shocking and devastating – it is unthinkable that the tremendous loss and grief could be made worse by the loss of another family member in the same way.

Thirty-six-year-old Pat Buckley from Midleton in Co. Cork buried two of his brothers within less than one and a half years. He witnessed a family with six children become a family with just four between June 2002 and September 2003.

The Buckley family was horrified when 30-year-old Mark, the third oldest, died by suicide on 24 June 2002. Mark's death was completely unexpected and left the family utterly bewildered and shattered with grief.

Mark had seemed very happy. He had plenty of friends and Pat says he was always the life and soul of the party. All of the Buckley siblings got on extremely well. Pat recalls how you'd always find a couple of the brothers in one pub and another two in another pub on the same night. Work-wise everything was going really well for Mark – like a couple of his brothers, he had a good job in construction. On the home front, he had started a family – he lived with his girlfriend and had a three-year-old son. He was a keen soccer player and played with Midleton Football Club. On the whole, his life appeared to all to be normal and happy and free of any major problems or worries.

Although it is often pointed out that men are less inclined to discuss their problems, Mark would talk to Pat and was able to discuss difficulties that he came across in life: 'He would ask me for advice.' Pat does recognise the obvious difference between women and men, however, in terms of discussion topics – women are more likely to talk about their feelings and share their problems, which is considered a huge factor in the much higher suicide rate of males compared to females. 'Men are different – they talk more about football, hurling, sex and drink. Women are more likely to discuss problems.'

Mark died on a Monday at about 6.45 in the evening. 'I used to always meet him for a pint but he wasn't in the usual pub that evening, so I stayed there and got something to eat myself.' Then Pat got a call from his sister. 'She was very upset and said something had happened in the house.' Pat left the pub immediately with a friend and the two went up to Mark's house. They were greeted by the sight of Pat's youngest brother, James, who was 21 at the time. He was outside the house, sitting on a wall. As Pat recalls the terrible moments before he discovered his brother's suicide, his eyes glaze over with sadness: 'James was shaking and couldn't speak. I went in the front door and saw the stairs. Mark was hanging from the attic door. He was still warm.'

'It's a sight I'll never forget, but at least we did get to see him.' Pat's friend told him not to take his brother down. His brother James was still outside, in severe shock. Pat realised that he now had to inform the rest of the family and organise for Mark to be taken down. 'I contacted the Gardaí and the priest and rang my dad.' Pat stopped his 56-year-old father from going into the house – he wanted to spare him the trauma of the harrowing scene. 'Mum was on holidays in Portugal. We had to bring her back home.' When his mother arrived back, she started apologising to all the family. 'She felt it was her fault.' The priest arrived and did the last rites for Mark and he was removed to the funeral home. Family and friends called over to the house to sympathise and support Mark's siblings and parents.

Mark had been in good form in the period preceding his death. 'It was a total shock. Something you wouldn't even suspect of Mark.' Pat says that, looking back, certain things could now be understood to be indicators that Mark had been planning to take his life, but they were signs that the family had not seen and only became known in the aftermath of his death. 'We found out that he had been with a friend of his a while before he died and when they were going, his friend said, "See you in two weeks," and Mark replied, "You won't be seeing me again." Signs such as these are so subtle they may be nothing other than throw-away, meaningless comments; though in the context of Mark's death, he clearly meant what he said.

Another factor that indicated Mark had been planning his death was the fact that he had paid up all his bills apart from just one last payment on the car. It appeared he had had it planned for at least six weeks. Pat took over his finances when he died. This was particularly difficult, especially when the bank continued to send letters looking for interest on Mark's mortgage. 'I sent the newspaper cuttings of his death to the bank, as they kept charging compound interest. It was just a computer formality.' Pat couldn't do anything with Mark's finances until they received an official certificate of death pending the inquest. 'We couldn't do anything about paying the mortgage. The ESB and Bord Gáis were okay about it. Eventually we sold the house and paid the compound interest and the mortgage.'

Pat and his parents went to the hospital to officially identify Mark. Six months later they had to attend the inquest, which, although they felt it was handled well, was very upsetting for them all. 'It was very professional. We all attended: cousins, in-laws, parents. Everyone was very sympathetic.' They learned that Mark had died by asphyxiation and his death was officially recorded as suicide. The inquest revealed that Mark had had a few pints the night he died. 'There were no drugs involved. He'd had a few pints but not a huge amount.'

Following the inquest, the family remained bewildered about the reasons Mark had taken his life. They were consumed by feelings of guilt and wondered why Mark had not come to them to talk about whatever was bothering him. 'Mark had no history of depression or psychiatric illness, and there is no history of it in the family. He had no physical illness, either.' Actually seeing his brother in the house after he died is something that stays with Pat. 'I wouldn't go through an attic door afterwards. Now I've moved house.'

The effects on the youngest brother, James, who found Mark, were particularly worrying. James had always been a happy-go-lucky type and had a good job as a spray-painter, but following Mark's death he started to have problems at work. 'He wasn't concentrating at work. He was drinking more than he usually did. When he started to go into depression, we started to worry about him. We brought James to the doctor. I don't know if the doctor put him on anti-depressants; and he also went to see a counsellor in the hospital.'

Professionals recommend that the person who discovers a death by suicide be watched closely afterwards as the emotional effects can put that person at particular risk. 'We had been advised by a psychologist friend to keep an eye on James and we were watching him like a hawk.' James was showing no signs of improving and even stopped being involved in sport.

Then, one day, Pat was particularly frightened by James's behaviour. 'One evening, our mother wasn't at home and he came bursting into my aunt's house, who lived next door. He was bawling crying and hysterical. He had been in the pub, but had only had two pints. He remembered walking down the road and passing a particular wall, where he saw a mirror reflection from the other side of the gate and he was convinced it wasn't his, but Mark's.' James's behaviour terrified Pat and he was extremely concerned about him. 'After Mark's death, James had promised Mum he'd never take his life.'

Prior to Mark's death, James had had no history of depression. 'When Mark died, it had an awful effect on James.' Pat says it's very difficult to see your own flesh and blood die, 'especially when you know it was their own choice'. There was no sign of James improving after a couple of months. The family were concerned about what James might do and tried to keep him in sight at all times. 'We watched him during the day and at weekends.'

Then, things appeared to be improving. James had a new girlfriend and was moving into an apartment with her. He had a child as well. 'Everything was going flying.'

Then, what the family had most dreaded did happen. James took his life on Sunday, 14 September 2003. 'On the Sunday morning I was at home. I had been out the night before. My uncle and cousin called to the house and I knew something was wrong.'

Pat, while we talk, maintains a matter-of-fact tone of voice and remains composed, but as he describes the moment that he found out he had lost a second brother to suicide, the tears start to come: 'They said, "It's James – he's in the regional, in the morgue." They were crying. I was crying.'

Pat went into overdrive. 'I had to tell my mother and my father. My uncle and cousin went to the Garda barracks. My mother was in Portugal on holidays again – this time, they contacted Interpol. My mother was on the phone in 20 minutes and was flown straight back to Dublin and got a lift home to Midleton. My mother knew what had happened the moment she received the call in Portugal. I was back to arranging the funeral.' James had died in his new apartment. Pat hated having to tell other family members the tragic news. 'I hated telling my sister about James. She carries the two boys' cards in her wallet.'

It was hard to fathom that they had lost another family member to suicide and had to go through all the agony they had experienced less than a year and a half ago all over again. In James's case, the family are still left wondering about the details surrounding his death, as they never got to hear the inquest, something which Pat is still very bitter about.

The inquest was held 12 months to the day after James's death. 'We arrived at the courthouse at a quarter past ten. The inquest was scheduled for twenty past ten, but when we arrived, we were told the inquest was over as there was a mix-up with the files, so we had missed it. We got nothing.' Pat was absolutely furious: 'I don't even know if there was drink taken. I know nothing and it makes me very bitter.'

Pat had to face all of the same painful events that he had gone through after Mark's death. 'We had to clean James's house out. I broke down inside the house. It was very hard.' Pat kept small mementoes of his brothers for himself. Their girlfriends kept little things like lighters and rings. There was very little to sort out for James; at 22 years of age, he was barely a man. 'I burned Mark's clothes. I didn't want anyone else to have them. We dug ourselves into serious debt. We'd so many funerals that we were all depressed – not going to work, drinking heavily. It had a domino effect.'

Apart from the loved ones directly bereaved by the deaths of Mark and James, there were knock-on effects on a huge number of others. 'There is the knock-on effect on wives and neighbours and friends. It tore everyone apart. Everyone is different, everyone has their own way of dealing with it.' Pat says that had he not had children, he would have escaped, gone away from it all to England. He knew he was hurting his wife. 'I would have gone to England and I know I'd have become an alcoholic.'

Both James and Mark left suicide notes, apologising for taking their lives but leaving no explanation as to why. The messages were simply messages of love and to say sorry.

Pat's parents were still thinking who would be next after James. He said he was reluctant to talk about it with his parents. 'With most problems, a problem shared is a problem halved, but not suicide. How can you talk to your mother about it when she's already worried about you?' Still, Pat says his mother is very strong: 'She smoked all her life, but packed it in when the boys died. My father thinks it's God getting back at him for all the years, but now sees it as a quest that he is working on and feels he can do something if he can save another life.'

The brothers did talk about it among themselves, including James before he died. 'We cried, we hugged ...' Pat would cry in public, but didn't want to upset his wife. 'I was just going out drinking, then home, then work. I had no other life. Every three months or so, I'd just say "F*** it". Sometimes I'm crying coming up the road. I have got a lot more soft, which has helped a lot. I talk about it more and cry in front of people, especially if I hear a song that was played at the funeral.'

The deaths of the boys had a heartbreaking effect on the family, but it did keep the Buckley family very close and they became stronger. Still, birthdays, Christmas, football matches and anniversaries are hard. 'The night Liverpool won the Champions League, we were still very hurt and very bitter. It's always very hard imagining what they'd be like if they were there. They'll never go away.' Some occasions can pose particular difficulties. 'My kids' godfathers were Mark and James. There is a dilemma in my mind at Communions, I wonder do I leave a blank seat in their place. These are the small things people don't think about.' He even feels that some people regarded them as criminals, which he says was a disgrace, and a factor that can make it very difficult for bereaved families in search of help. 'There was a stigma. It did feel like some friends avoided us, they didn't know what to say.'

Pat has noticed a remarkable change in society's attitude as suicide becomes less and less of a taboo subject. 'The stigma is going now.' Pat says that now you see posters going up in public places with information and contact numbers for counsellors who deal with suicide bereavement. He said, in the past, everyone acted as though a person who died by suicide was a criminal. He recalls the first funeral home that they brought Mark to. Pat says they showed no respect for his body and did not even fix his clothes or lay him properly in the coffin, and the family immediately brought him to another funeral home.

Pat says the anger is now gone. 'People can be so embarrassed by suicide in their family. I feel they should be proud of the life they [the person who died] lived before they died. After my brothers died, some of the community found it very hard to talk to us.'

Pat feels there is no point in trying to understand why his brothers took their lives. 'Why do people kill themselves? Mark was an A student, always looking to make a joke. We'd a good quality of life. Mark had a son he adored. There's no point in asking *Why*? I asked *Why*? for a long time, but you're only torturing yourself.' Pat says the loss of his brothers to suicide used to madden him. 'Now it saddens me.'

Following the death of the two brothers, two good friends of the family – Garda Pat Organ and Mark Lynch – organised a meeting to see if something could be done about the high levels of suicide. Out of this grew the Let's Get Together Foundation, which aims to help others affected by suicide and to look at ways of preventing it. Following the huge amount of work he has done in this area, Pat believes that Mark must have been suffering from some kind of depression, some type of chemical imbalance, to make him do what he did.

When Mark died the family began to understand what a big issue suicide was. The Garda who came to the scene of the death said that it was the third suicide he had come across in the space of just one month. Pat began thinking of measures they could take to help other families who had lost people to suicide; he got great help from the local Gardaí in this. 'The Gardaí were fabulous throughout the circumstances surrounding Mark's death. A Garda friend and another friend met my Dad to talk about a soccer tournament, a charity soccer match for the organisation called Friends of the Suicide Bereaved in Cork. They played football and raised nearly €7,000.' The Garda friend suggested that the Buckley family could do something similar and Pat organised a group of friends to play a football match to raise funds in Midleton.

In June 2005, the Let's Get Together Foundation linked up with a number of similar organisations throughout the country to set up All-Ireland Suicide Prevention. They all sat down together to see what they could do to help prevent suicide and help people bereaved by the loss of a loved one to suicide. They decided that the first thing to do was raise awareness of the issue and so they spoke to local and national media.

Pat now wants to see a centre set up locally in which they can start to bring about some change. 'There are about 21 other families in the town who have lost people to suicide. We would love to help them, but we can't do it if we don't have a centre. We need the resources.' He is currently campaigning for a centre not only to deal directly with the suicide bereaved, but also to provide young people with a safe environment where they can talk to others.

'If you put people into a non-drug, non-alcohol centre, people will know when they are happy and when they are not happy. It will give individuals the opportunity to bond and talk. If kids don't play sport and don't have money, they have nothing to do after 6 pm.'

Pat feels there are significant pressures on the youth of today. 'Things were so different in the past. If you robbed an orchard when I was a kid, you got a kick up the ass, now you get a summons. It's the system.' The Let's Get Together Foundation want to see a pilot scheme set up in a couple of counties in Ireland. He says a couple of million euro would provide the funds for a centre and would offer something positive. 'There's no youth club or meeting place for young people outside sports facilities. We need an open-house centre, a drop-in centre. If someone is having a bad day, they can have a friendly chat and a cup of tea, a centre run by youth for the youth. That way they would be given a sense of responsibility for the town and for themselves. The youth are the future of tomorrow.'

Pat says it's time for the government to promote and support such initiatives. 'Local businesses are great, but you can only ask them for so much. Why do lay people have to do it when it's a health board issue? The government is failing the people.'

To date, the Let's Get Together Foundation has done a huge amount of fundraising. 'We have got computers and have done a huge amount of research. We also keep in regular contact with other organisations.' Together with other organisations, they act as a lobby group. Pat is convinced that the levels of suicide in Ireland are higher than reported, due to the stigma attached and also for insurance reasons. 'If you don't leave a suicide note, it can be reported as death by misadventure.'

The Let's Get Together Foundation also acts as a referral service. 'If anybody contacts us, such as a person worried about another person or someone who is suicidal themselves, we contact a counsellor who'll contact the person and assess who they need. We then set up an appointment with them for as soon as possible.' The Let's Get Together Foundation uses funds raised to pay for the first sessions automatically. All calls are treated in strict confidentiality and everything is anonymous. Counsellors employed are private counsellors. Pat feels that the immediate service they organise is crucial. From the first phone call to the Let's Get Together

Foundation to the first appointment takes just 45 minutes. 'Through the system, it would be 44 days.'

One year after the foundation of the Let's Get Together Foundation in 2004, the organisation had received approximately 1,200 calls, which is indicative of the seriousness of the problem.

The organisation now wants to see the government take action. 'We would like the government to get up and address the issue realistically and stop spending all of the money on research. We need quick [assessment] of situations. You need to be seen straight away.' Pat also feels that the gap between mental services for children and adults needs to be addressed. Mental health services for children do not include 16- and 17-year-olds; they fall into the adult category. 'It's a disgrace to see 16-year-olds going into psychiatric wards with 40- and 50-year-olds who are mentally disturbed. It's frightening.'

Pat feels the work carried out by the Let's Get Together Foundation has made a difference in the Midleton area, though he points out there is still a huge amount of work to be done. 'Suicide is still happening.'

Mark and James are survived by their mother and father and brothers, Pat, Neil and Phillip and sister Louise.

If you need someone to talk to, you can contact the Let's Get Together Foundation at 087 691 7609 or you can email patbuckleylgtf@yahoo.co.uk.

Bryan Walsh

Eighteen-year-old Bryan Walsh from Enfield in Co. Meath took his own life on 17 August 2003. The Walsh family was hit by complete and utter shock when they learned that their successful, easy-going, beloved son had taken his own life.

The family had seen no signs whatsoever that Bryan had problems in the period prior to his death. Bryan, being the baby of the family, was doted on by the others, and adored for his cheeky sense of humour and great sense of fun. Furthermore, Bryan was in a loving relationship with his girlfriend, Gemma, and the couple had a two-year-old daughter, Kaelah, to whom Bryan was utterly devoted.

The family constantly recall the days preceding Bryan's death in an attempt to pick up on any sign that something was amiss, but he had been in the best of form. His mother, Anne, had picked her son up from the bus from his college in Dundalk two days before. They both got on very well and went into Enfield for a drink to catch up. They talked about plans for that evening. Bryan had received a text from Gemma to see if they were going to join her at a 21st birthday party they had all been invited to, so Bryan and Anne went off to join her. All went well and the next day life continued as normal.

Anne went shopping and Bryan was busy building a Wendy house for his beloved Kaelah. He had even good-humouredly warned the whole family not to 'let Daddy near it'. Both Bryan and his father, Tom, were good with their hands and there was friendly competition between them; Bryan always liked to finish a job he had started.

Bryan's sister, 24-year-old Shirley, who is the eldest in the family, was distraught at the loss of her baby brother to suicide. The two had always been very close and Shirley was crazy about Bryan and his little daughter, Kaelah. She was always on hand to help Bryan out and was delighted to spend time with Kaelah and mind her. The night Bryan died, Shirley had come over before Bryan went out to take Kaelah for a walk. The last time she saw Bryan was when she was leaving with Kaelah in the buggy. She told her beloved brother to enjoy himself and have a good night out.

That evening, Gemma and Bryan were going out together and Anne and Tom were minding Kaelah. Bryan had told his Mum before going out not to bath his little girl as he would do it the following day. He was a very responsible father and didn't even want his mother to have to change his daughter's nappy. Anne gave Bryan a lift into town where he hooked up with Gemma. His brother Tomas met up with him for a drink as well. They all had a great time and the great conversations they were having kept them out until around 5 am. Gemma went to her house and Bryan back to his family home. What happened next remains a tragic mystery for Gemma and the whole Walsh family.

Byran's father, Tom, got up at a quarter to eight on the Sunday morning and noticed that the garden shed door was open. He immediately saw his son inside and hurried in. 'I wasn't sure whether it was 22-year-old Tomas or 18-year-old Bryan as they look very alike. I was stunned for a minute. I then called my daughter Shirley's boyfriend, Shane, and rang the sergeant in Kilcock, who came out straight away. He arranged a priest, a doctor, everything, all of whom knew Bryan. We didn't want a stranger.' Their son Tomas, who is now 23, was not in the house and he received the phone call at around five minutes to eight, just after Bryan had been found. The devastating aftermath of the discovery of Bryan's body signified the worst time in the Walsh family's life. Bryan's body was brought to hospital and his father, Tom, identified him. They got him home on Monday. His mother wanted to bring his body back to the house. 'I didn't want him to go straight down to the church.'

As the reality of Bryan's death sunk in, the family were bewildered and confused. They couldn't for a moment fathom how Bryan could have been so desperate that he felt compelled to take his own life. Bryan was an electrician and was doing an apprenticeship. He excelled as an electrician and, only one month before he died, his boss had suggested that he should do the guild exam. Siblings and parents would often meet up socially. 'Normally, every Saturday night, myself and Tom would go out as well and we'd all hook up. We'd often hook up with the kids.' His three siblings, Debbie, Shirley and Tomas, got on exceptionally well. They recall how they would all text each other on an evening out and frequently end up getting a taxi home together. 'If something bothers us in our family, we come right out with it.' He also treasured evenings in with Gemma: 'Bryan wouldn't go out that often. The two of us would regularly stay in together. We'd just hang out – maybe get a Chinese take-away,' she recalls.

What was particularly baffling was the fact that Bryan had already gone through all the difficult stuff: Gemma being pregnant and his Leaving Certificate. Kaelah was born during his exams. He was a happy-go-lucky type. His family say he was a big messer: 'Bryan was always having a laugh. He had a great sense of humour.' Tomas recalls the bank holiday weekend before Bryan died. The brothers were having a cigarette and a friend of theirs who was a Garda was getting impatient and wanted to move on to the pub. Bryan held up his hands as if to be handcuffed and asked, 'What are you going to do – arrest me?' His sister Debbie describes the laugh Bryan would have with Tomas: 'One evening I was coming home in a taxi with Tomas and he was on the phone to Bryan. They were joking about something that they obviously both found hilarious. They weren't even talking, just cracking up laughing and Tomas was hammering the dashboard so much so that the taxi driver had to tell him to stop. It was all harmless fun.' Bryan got on with everyone. He had absolutely no enemies. 'He was totally laid-back and friendly to everyone – he wouldn't say anything hurtful to anyone.'

Bryan could do anything with his hands. His father remembers Bryan's determination. 'If Bryan was going to do something, he'd do it. With Bryan there was no such thing as an attempt. He was very determined, even stubborn. He'd have his way. We were out there in the garden one Saturday and I was carrying heavy stuff in out of the boot and Bryan said, "Da, I bet you I could lift one of those," and he brought it over. He was as strong as anything.' Tomas remembers how Bryan was always making things: 'He used to make little tractors out of cigarette boxes. He had a great life and plenty of hobbies. He was very into music and played the guitar. He particularly liked the music of Damien Rice, who, as it happened, was Gemma's cousin.

What Bryan said and did the weekend of his death gave no indication that he was planning to take his life. On the day before his death, he had arranged a lift back up to college for the Sunday morning. Gemma says he was in good form in the pub on the evening before. In conversation that night, he had even mentioned that he had a nixer to do the following day in Enfield. Added to this, he had told his mother only the day before not to bath his daughter because he was going to do it. He had had a great time with Gemma on the Saturday evening – they talked about everything. The family now believe that the alcohol Bryan drank on the Saturday night could hold the key to his shocking suicide.

He had drunk a lot that night. Gemma estimates he probably drank at least ten vodkas mixed with an energy drink. The family has now learned that alcohol, rather than being a stimulant, is a depressant. The combination of chemicals appears to have had a drastic effect on Bryan's mind. Bryan stopped drinking at 2 am and a few hours later, his family believe he hit a low as a result of the chemicals and entered a very dark place. This will be discussed in a later chapter.

Tragically, Bryan was one of nine or ten young people (all but one of whom were men) who have died by suicide in the Kilcock parish in recent years. One of them included a close friend of Bryan's and it had made Bryan very angry. Parish priest Fr P.J. suggested that the family hold a candle service for Bryan and they saw this as an opportunity to speak to other young people out there, to let them know that suicide was not the way, that there were other solutions. 'We were very worried about copy-cat suicides.' They put gazebos up outside the house: one with Bryan's guitar, the other with a photograph of the tragic teenager. Gemma's cousin, singer Damien Rice, turned up to play at the service. 'He came from the heart and played off his own bat. Bryan was mad about Damien. He was always trying to get the others to be fans.' Tomas and Debbie say he would text them when there were pieces about the singer in the paper. 'We had amplifiers outside and were using microphones. We wanted to tell young people if they were in trouble to seek help.' The family expected about 30 people to turn up – instead there were hundreds. Bryan was laid out in Tomas's room. Fr P.J. asked Bryan's mother to read a prayer that had been in his room.

'I had a piece of paper and a prayer in my hand. I knew I had to speak without crying. I said the few words. When the ceremony was finished, we brought candles out to the gazebo – there were 500, 600, maybe 700 people outside, all holding candles. It was the most unbelievable sight you could ever see. The people were shoulder to shoulder. It took at least an hour before the last person had placed their candle on the gazebo.' Fr P.J. realised that it would never be easy to get that many 18–20-year-olds together again. 'He never went to bed all night. He was very straight and very strong to them. With that age group, you have to be very careful. Fr P.J. said suicide was not the way to do it – he named the Samaritans and Aware.' Bryan's brothers and sisters delivered a eulogy at the funeral mass to tell people what Bryan was really like – that his suicide was the result of a moment of madness, influenced by the mixture of chemicals Bryan had consumed that fateful night.

The pain of Bryan's death will never disappear. The shed where his body was found has since been demolished. His mother is still at a loss to understand the reasons behind the suicide: 'Bryan's death really appears to have been a moment of madness. I don't think anything as bad will ever happen again. Bryan would never have done this to any of us. The aftermath on the family is horrific. It's so hard for anyone losing a child, but suicide has to be the hardest. You can't blame anything – if you at least have something to lash out at, and of course you feel guilt ... you remember every time you had a row. You ask yourself had he something on his mind, could he have talked to you. Bryan is the first and last thing you think of each day. We will never, ever forget this but the pain will ease with time. I still get a bang in my chest every day.'

'We're getting on as a family because we talk about it. We talk about him when we're out. No one is afraid to say Bryan's name because we talk about it so much. Time means nothing. The shock goes. The pain never ceases. The family will never be the same again. The saddest part is that he had so much in front of him – it was such a waste of life. Once you can talk, I think it is important. Family, friends and neighbours were second to none. They were brilliant.'

Bryan's daughter, Kaelah, is now three years old. The last thing he said to Kaelah was 'You're such a clever little girl'. The family makes sure not to let Kaelah see them upset. 'Kaelah is our only grandchild. I don't know what we would have done without her. We have now made Bryan's room into a room for Gemma and Kaelah. She sees it as her room and even tells Debbie to remove her shoes from there! Recently she said, "I miss my Daddy."' Kaelah visits Bryan's grave – 'Daddy's garden' – and goes over and kisses his photo. 'There are two Irish flags on it now because Kaelah wouldn't let us take down the one from Paddy's Day last year.'

They now try to concentrate on Kaelah and all of the good memories. His mum treasures the memories of his gentleness: 'When I was ill, I remember when he was little and I was lying down in bed, he'd put the head around and say, "Ma, are you alright? Would you like a cup of tea?", and before I could get a word in edgeways he'd say, "I know, I know ... very little milk and two sugars". He was a real little charmer. He was also a showman. The kids prepared breakfast one morning years ago when they were young. Bryan was about six and he had painted on a moustache like a butler and acted the butler. They were all so close in years and grew up very fast. Life will never be the same.' Gemma nods. 'What can you do? You don't know why it happens.'

Alcohol and Suicide

Bryan Walsh's story raises the general question of what role alcohol plays in suicidal behaviour. In a number of the personal stories in this book, the individual who died by suicide had drunk alcohol at the time of taking their life. In the case of the River Foyle (see Chapter 16), Foyle Search and Rescue identified nights when people were out socialising and drinking, i.e. Thursday, Friday and Saturday nights, as the times when they were most likely to encounter suicide and attempted suicide. Indeed, Foyle Search and Rescue volunteers report that 99 per cent of individuals that they have come across climbing over the bridge railings or that they have rescued from the waters of the Foyle River have consumed alcohol; the majority of these incidents occurred after the pubs and clubs had closed.

Still, the connection between alcohol and suicide is complex: it does not simply relate to whether the individual was intoxicated at the actual time of taking his or her life.

Alcohol can be related to suicide in terms of reducing a person's inhibitions to the extent that they carry out the act. As a depressant, it can also alter a person's mood, producing feelings of anxiety or depression the same night, the following day or even a number of days later; that low mood can be significant enough to create suicidal thoughts. Alcohol can also be disinhibiting, thereby allowing someone to do something that they may think but never do. *The Aware Commissioned Report on Alcohol and Suicide: Interim findings* (2004) states that although people generally think about alcohol-induced disinhibition as being associated with exuberant or reckless behaviour, this disinhibition can be associated with more negative behaviour at times. The report explains, 'If a young man is depressed, goes on a binge-drinking session and gets more depressed, he may become disinhibited enough to act suicidally, where he wouldn't when sober.'

In 45 per cent of suicides, alcohol is implicated for one or more reasons, according to Dr John Connolly, Secretary of the Irish Association of Suicidology (IAS). Dr Connolly says that, apart from the fact that alcohol can reduce a person's inhibitions to the extent that they may carry out the act, there have been instances in which the family and friends of a person who took his or her life while intoxicated are convinced that suicide would not have crossed the person's mind if they hadn't been drunk.

As suicide is also strongly related to depression, and as alcohol increases depression, the substance can play a significant role in affecting the mood of a suicidal individual. Suicide rates are high among chronic alcoholics and research from the UK lists alcoholics among the groups most at risk, with the risk multiplied by an estimated 20 times when compared with the general population. Alcoholism is associated with high rates of depressive disorders and according to Dr Connolly, 'People believe alcohol is a stimulant, whereas in reality it's a depressant.' Indeed, the interim report from Aware draws attention to significant research which shows that suicidality was disproportionately greater than other psychiatric symptoms in depressed alcoholics.

At a 2005 Dáil debate on the issue, President of the IAS, Dan Neville TD, stated that alcohol consumption led to depression, which is a major factor in suicide and suicidal behaviour. 'In addition, depressed persons frequently turn to alcohol in the mistaken belief it will improve their mood. In many people alcohol has a biphasic effect, initially causing a feeling of well-being but soon to be followed by dysphoria.' With up to 90 per cent of suicides associated with mental illness, such as depression, the connection between alcohol and depressed moods is, thus, significant.

The increase in suicide in Ireland in recent years has occurred in tandem with the rising rate of alcohol consumption. Between 1960 and 2000, consumption of alcohol per adult over 15 years of age had risen from almost 5 litres to 14 litres of pure alcohol. In the same period, suicide rates had gone from an average of 64 to an average of over 450 annually. In the ten years from 1989 to 1999, alcohol consumption in Ireland rose by a massive 40 per cent.

This period showed a parallel increase of 45 per cent in the suicide rate in Ireland, particularly among young people. Speaking at the Third Annual Conference of the IAS centred on alcohol and substance misuse and suicidal behaviour, Dr Connolly pointed out that 'Among our European partners, Ireland is the only country where youth suicide rates continue to rise. In most of our neighbours, rates of alcohol consumption have fallen, as have the suicide rates.'

At the 2005 Dáil Debate, Dan Neville TD said that the alarming increase in suicide incidence in Ireland, particularly among young people, is exactly mirrored by a graph showing the increase in alcohol consumption from 1972 to 2000. He said alcohol abuse is a significant risk factor in suicide and compounds other risk factors.

He also referred to a clear association between the per capita consumption of alcohol and the suicide rate in any country. 'The higher the level of consumption of alcohol, the higher the suicide rate. Alcohol consumption levels can explain the difference in suicide rates between countries and between different areas in each country.'

This theory was borne out when Gorbachev introduced an anti-alcohol abuse campaign in the Soviet Union in the 1980s, which resulted in a significant drop in the suicide rates. Professor Keith Hawton says, 'The campaign included increasing detection and treatment of alcohol abuse patterns, as well as reducing availability of alcohol. The suicide rate rose rapidly once their campaign ended.' Although Professor Hawton points out that there were other changes going on in the Soviet Union in the late 1980s, which may also have been relevant to the suicide rate, he believes that the Soviet Union example provides hope that the problem of alcohol abuse and suicide can be tackled with some hope of success.

The correlation between the rise in alcohol consumption and deaths by suicide, especially among groups which are identified as increasing their alcohol intake, has caused concern. Of particular note is the increase in alcohol consumption among young women, against the backdrop of a significant rise in suicide among this group.

Suicide rates among young women aged 15–24 doubled over a 10-year period from the early 1990s, while the overall rate of suicide for women remained stable, which could reflect the change in drinking patterns among other things. Dr John Connolly says 'Traditionally one of the protective factors against suicide in women has been the low rates of alcohol abuse, less than one fifth that of men. The interim report of the strategy group on alcohol shows that at risk drinking in that age group in Ireland is now higher than that of men.'

At the 2003 IAS Conference on Alcohol and Suicide, Dr Justin Brophy referred to a study from the UK, which indicated that the increased rate of suicide in young women is related to an increase in alcohol consumption. An *Evening Herald* article of 16 August 2005 stated that more men than women are treated for alcohol abuse, representing a reversal of traditional trends. The article referred to the European School Survey Project on Alcohol and Other Drugs, which stated that Irish teenage *females* remain the biggest 'binge drinkers' in Europe. The Aware commissioned report on alcohol and suicide states that binge drinking has been shown by researchers to be associated with completed suicide, as opposed to other drinking patterns which are associated with uncompleted suicide attempts. Of the 86 females who took their lives in 2003, 18 were under the age of 25 and 38 were under the age of 35.

Ivan J. Perry also suggests in the 2002 report by the National Parasuicide Registry that the increase in alcohol consumption levels observed in the past decade in Ireland have accentuated the already high rates of deliberate self-harm in young women. 'The findings on alcohol are consistent with the considerable evidence from the national and international literature that alcohol is an important risk and facilitating factor associated with suicidal behaviour.'

Dr Brophy points out that both the female and the adolescent body can only metabolise alcohol at half the rate of the adult male, making these groups more at risk of toxic consequences.

Still, the rate of male suicide is four times greater than the female suicide rate in Ireland and is particularly high among young men. Indeed, suicide is the biggest cause of death in men aged between 15 and 24 years. Out of a total of 444 suicides in Ireland in 2003, 358 were men, 94 were under the age of 25 and 175 were under the age of 34. Dr John Owens refers to recent studies which indicate that there has been a substantial increase in drinking in Irish teenagers, with the 'typical binge-drinking characteristics of young drinkers'. Dr Justin Brophy says that the European School Survey Project on Alcohol and Other Drugs indicates that Ireland is top of the league of under-age drinkers, with three-quarters of 15- and 16-year-olds drinking alcohol at least once a month and one-third of them admitting to binge drinking on three or more occasions a month. He also stresses that under-age drinkers are susceptible to acute consequences of alcohol use 'including blackouts, hangovers and alcohol poisoning'. Brophy says that adolescents need only drink half as much to suffer the same negative effects as adults, and there is significant evidence of damage to brain regions, particularly areas that affect learning and memory.

Speaking at the 2005 STOP Conference on Suicide, Rev. Dr Tony Byrne spoke of an 'acute darkness in the middle of the night' identified by The Irish College of General Practitioners. 'This is associated with *young people*. Alcohol and [the drug] ecstasy are often associated with this acute darkness.' Indeed the 2003 Conference heard that Ireland had the second highest rate of suicide among young males. Prof. Ad Kerkhof said, 'The drinking of young people, especially binge drinking, in order to become unconscious is dangerous [...] Young people who do so have emotional problems. We should never take this as normal. It is extremely abnormal.'

Dan Neville also pointed out that the lifetime risk for suicide in alcoholism is thought to be between 3 per cent and 7 per cent and the risk for major depressive illness is approximately 15 per cent. 'The comorbidity of depression and alcohol abuse greatly increases the risk of suicide and suicidal behaviour.'

At the 2003 IAS Conference on Alcohol and Suicide, Dr John Owens explained that the connection between alcohol and suicide is associated with social disruption and also major loss events, such as the loss of employment and the break-up of relationships. This point emphasises how alcohol per se cannot be blamed directly for suicide, but how it relates to a complex of factors which together can bring on suicidal thoughts in an individual. Indeed, Dr Justin Brophy points out that while there is evidence documenting the link between alcohol and suicide 'correlation is not causation'. He says that acute effects of alcohol such as reduced inhibition, increased aggression, change in behaviour, as well as emotional and perceptual distortion and exacerbated lowered mood are significant in facilitating suicidal acts.

It is also of note that as well as being associated with fatal suicidal behaviour, alcohol is strongly associated with non-fatal suicidal behaviour. The 2002 report of the National Parasuicide Registry in Ireland found that for a total of 42 per cent of all episodes of parasuicide (non-fatal suicidal behaviour) registered in 2002, there was evidence of alcohol consumption before the act of parasuicide.

Ivan J. Perry, Professor of Epidemiology and Public Health at University College Cork, said that while the proportion of men who consumed alcohol as part of the act was higher than that of women – 46.1 per cent, as compared to 38.6 per cent – there is evidence that alcohol is an increasingly important factor in parasuicide by women, which may reflect broader trends in alcohol consumption in Ireland.

In 2003, the Third Annual Conference of the IAS centred on alcohol and substance misuse and suicidal behaviour. Speaking on the nature of the association between alcohol and suicidal behaviour, Professor Keith Hawton stressed that substance use increases vulnerability to suicidal behaviour. One reason is that 'substance misuse eventually leads on to depression, which leads on to suicidal thinking and suicidal behaviour. The association may reflect the fact that both substance abuse and suicidal behaviour may share underlying common risk factors.' He also confirmed in his presentation that substance use reduces immediate thresholds for suicidal behaviour. Indeed, he pointed out that when comparing suicidal intent scores, it was found that those who were drinking at the time of self-harm had a lower suicidal intent score overall than those who did not drink at the time of self-harm. 'So substance use, especially alcohol misuse, is likely to increase impulsivity, narrow the focus of a person's psychological awareness and can particularly impair problem-solving [...] Alcohol, and probably drug misuse, may greatly increase the danger of suicidal acts.'

Clearly, alcohol itself can not be cited as an independent cause of suicide. Alcohol has always played an important part of social life in societies throughout the world and Hawton points to the possibility that part of the association between alcohol and suicide is due to sharing common underlying risk factors: 'We know that traumatic or adverse childhood experiences are common both in people who abuse alcohol and in those engaging in suicidal behaviour; the same is true of family dysfunction.'

What are the common factors that cause people to abuse alcohol and have suicidal thoughts? The one thing alcohol and suicide have in common is that they are both about altering consciousness. Dr John Connolly says people in crisis can turn to both in order to ease the pain. 'They feel they must alter the pain.' Professor Keith Hawton says that both alcohol and suicide 'change the consciousness of worrying, negative thoughts, negative feelings, anxiety and stress'.

It's not just the person who abuses alcohol who is at risk, indeed alcohol misuse in an individual may also lead to an increase in suicide risk in people around them because of the effects of alcohol on family function, particularly through associations with domestic violence and physical and sexual abuse. Another connection between alcohol and suicide arises through the health consequences of alcohol abuse, such as liver cirrhosis, heart disease, accidents and severe injuries, putting these individuals into another group at risk of suicide.

What is of particular note in the discussion on the connection between alcohol and suicide is the repeated reference to the fact that the rate of alcohol consumption has risen so significantly in Ireland and thus raises the question: why are Irish people, and particularly young Irish people, drinking more and more?

The report on alcohol and suicide commissioned by Aware points to four main causes: increased disposable income, highly liberal licensing and regulation laws, an alcohol permissive culture and significant expenditure by the drinks industry on the promotion of drinking, particularly in relation to young people.

The pharmacological reasons that people drink alcohol are, according to Dr Justin Brophy, to lower anxiety, to take advantage of the sedative effects, to cheer up, to induce euphoria and increase self-esteem, to loosen up, to release inhibitions, to escape from our superego or conscience, to forget (exploiting alcohol's amnesiac effects) and to obtain oblivion. Still, Dr Brophy points out that in Ireland, these functions are often exploited through excessive use of alcohol. Dr Brophy argues that while Irish people use the traditional excuse of the political oppression caused by colonialism as the reason for alcohol excess, 'We have colonised ourselves with our alcohol mythology.'

Dr Brophy sees the globalised status of Ireland as contributing significantly to the massive increase in alcohol use and, indeed, abuse. 'Ireland is now the most globalised state in the world. This has the effect of dislocating ourselves somewhat from our traditional collective conscious.' He speaks of a breakdown in community and family, by individualism and a sense of living in the 'here and now'. 'These are strategies used to reconnect with our lost, romanticised past, largely through consumerism and alcohol.' He does subscribe to the old adage that 'there is nothing else to do in Ireland except go to the pub', which he says is to some extent true, considering the low level of investment in community alternatives.

In fact, this is an area that a huge number of organisations working to reduce suicide feel very strongly about. One of the primary aims of Pat Buckley of the Let's Get Together Foundation in Midleton, Cork, is to establish a community centre for young people. He feels that if young people can be in a non-drug, non-alcohol centre, people will know when they are happy and when they are not happy. He says if kids don't play sport and don't have money, they have nothing to do after 6 pm (See Chapter 9).

The Department of Health and Children have recognised the significant role of alcohol in suicidal behaviour and in the 10-year

National Strategy for Action on Suicide Prevention, launched in September 2005, alcohol and substance abuse was listed as one of 26 areas to target for action. The report states its objective as being 'to challenge permissive, harmful attitudes to alcohol abuse, help to reduce overall consumption rates and raise awareness of the association between alcohol and/or substance abuse and suicidal behaviour'.

The interim report from Aware recommends education, regulation and enforcement. The report states that the social, personal and health education curriculum, which is mandatory in all post-primary schools in Ireland, should encompass alcohol education. They also stress the need to increase awareness of the association between alcohol and suicide and the need to enforce the drinking laws stringently, with particular respect to the ban on serving underage drinkers and intoxicated customers. They believe there should be expenditure on alcohol awareness advertising equivalent to that of expenditure on alcohol promotional advertising. Indeed, there are a number of advertising awareness campaigns already in place which promote responsible drinking and highlight the negative effects of drinking; these are targeted at the high-risk teenage group.

Suicide and Schools

With the increasing rate of suicidality among young people in Ireland, schools have inevitably been affected, whether in terms of students having suicidal thoughts, attempting suicide or, in the worst and most extreme cases, losing a student to suicide. In 1980, the number of young people aged between 10 and 19 to die by suicide was 12; in recent years, that figure has risen considerably, to 37 in 2002. Interestingly, while in 1980 there were 3 deaths in the 10–14 age group, in 2002 there were none; so the figure of 37 suicides in 2002 encompasses individuals aged between 15 and 19 only. This means that the problem of student suicide is more likely to affect a secondary school. Although very few schools in Ireland will ever be faced with an actual student suicide, there is a massive increase in the rate of suicide among young people in Ireland in the five to six years after leaving school. Among 15–24-year-olds, Ireland has the fifth highest rate of suicide in the European Union.

Experts believe that schools have an important role to play in recognising at-risk students and helping them to cope with their problems. They believe that the promotion of positive mental health at school will assist young people in coping with life's challenges, both while they are at school and, later, as young adults. The National Health Development Agency warns that suicidal behaviour is established early on in life and such behaviour in schools may prefigure an actual suicide. It is thus a priority that schools develop a programme to recognise such behaviour and work with the students in order to treat the problem. Dr John Connolly of the Irish Association of Suicidology highlights the crucial role that schools must play in the early identification of young people at risk and in promoting positive mental health generally. 'Building self-esteem and teaching problem-solving skills that enable young people to cope with the difficulties and disappointments of life are essential activities. This will go a long way towards reducing the tragedy of youth suicide and, in time, as we turn out citizens better able to cope with their lives, reduce the risk of suicide in later years.'

In *Suicide Awareness*, Dan Neville TD points out that in Ireland, in the 16–18 age bracket, the risk of suicide is higher among those who have dropped out of school than among those who have stayed on. Hence, it is also of critical importance for parents and teachers alike to work at keeping students in the educational environment until the cycle has been completed.

First and foremost in working towards suicide prevention at school level, is the need to create a coping, supportive and caring ethos in the school. The National Educational Psychological Service (NEPS) says schools should create a physically and psychologically safe school through the development of areas such as an anti-bullying policy, peer support programmes and suicide awareness programmes. The NEPS also highlights the need to include 'coping' programmes in the curriculum, covering such areas as communication skills, self-esteem, decision-making, bereavement and stress management.

Students, it seems, are crying out for such courses. In the story of the death of Darren Bolger (see Chapter 5), his mother, Maureen, told me that following Darren's death, his schoolmates told her that many of them worried about things and many admitted to contemplating suicide. She was horrified to learn that they did not know where to go for help. Maureen told me that she learned from the teenagers that matters that may appear trivial to an adult can be of huge importance to a teenager. Maureen expressed to me her conviction that more young people would be lost to suicide if awareness of the issue was not further raised in schools.

In early 2005, while researching an article for the *Evening Herald*, a 17-year-old girl told me that girls needed more 'coping-with-life' classes. She felt that there were huge pressures on them: the stress of exams, negative body image and eating disorders were among the problems facing her and her classmates and often they were at a loss as to what to do.

'Coping-with-life' classes are important in Irish schools today. According to Mrs Smith, a secondary school principal in the Eastern Health Board Region, there are more pressures on young people today than there were 30 or 40 years ago. 'In the past, the problems were physical – literally getting from A to B, but now they are psychological.' Mrs Smith says we are living in a materialistic society, where money is readily available but the institutions of family and religion have broken down. 'It is a very liberal society and young people are yearning for a spiritual life, but they don't seem to get it.' She says it is hard for students to find meaning when there are no restrictions any more. Feedback she has received also indicates that students are sexually active from as early as first year, at the age of 12 and 13, which adds to the emotional pressures they are under.

'Life has changed so fundamentally. Where we once had rules and regulations, you don't seem to have these any more. Life is now about materialism. We live in a consumer society. Then, there is the pressure of the [exam] points system. Everyone feels they have to go to university. An important message that we try to communicate to our students is that there is life beyond the Leaving Cert. If you don't get what you want first time around, you can always repeat, but you don't have to repeat either. Third level isn't the be-all and end-all of life – there are so many other options that can make you happy. Happiness is what is important in life – not points.'

Although Mrs Smith says there are a lot of positive elements in today's more liberal society, the fact that both parents now tend to go out to work leaves students, in her opinion, with too much freedom and too little supervision. Parents don't seem to have the same authority over their children nowadays. As a result of the competing influences of commercialism and the more liberal media, children tend to question and belittle their parents' opinions.

'They carry a lot of baggage into school. They may have boyfriend/girlfriend problems and problems at home and the level of problems affecting their well-being seems to have increased significantly in recent years.' Mrs Smith says that increased disposable income and the resulting increase in alcohol consumption is also having a huge effect on the students' well-being. 'A lot of parents do not know how much drink a lot of their children take. It's the done thing to go out to get drunk rather than go out to enjoy a few drinks. The result of heavy drinking at the weekend filters into the classroom and some students are frequently absent or in another world.'

Mrs Smith says the problem is particularly prevalent among female students. Indeed, experts believe that there may be a correlation between the increase in binge drinking among young women and the rise in the suicide rate for the same group. Experts point out that there are similar underlying causes to the abuse of alcohol and attempted suicide: each alters the consciousness of the person and can be perceived as offering relief from pain (see Chapter 11, Alcohol and Suicide).

Life skills classes are part of the curriculum in a number of schools, including that at which Mrs Smith is principal. 'These classes have been in place for a number of years now and are very important. Students are taught how to cope with problems and the ups and downs of life. They can also have one-to-one sessions with the school counsellor.' While Mrs Smith says it is difficult to instil self-esteem, they make every effort to promote it as a key element of these classes. 'We try to drill it home and assert the value and importance of each individual. The school has a strong role as a support service, even if it is not always in a classroom setting. Nowadays, students will come to teachers looking for support and advice with their problems and a year head is assigned to each class to give them this outlet.'

The NEPS suggest that schools create pastoral care structures and review their effectiveness. They also recommend that schools access training for staff to help them to deal with critical incidents, develop procedures for referral, and form links with outside agencies. Furthermore, they advise schools to establish a planning team in order to develop a critical incident management plan, so that they are prepared for crisis events.

It is also essential that teachers are aware of the signs of suicide risk in students, so that they can take appropriate action. The NEPS has published a resource pack called *Responding to Critical Incidents: Advice and Information Pack for Schools*, which includes a section to help teachers assess suicide potential. Teachers are advised that when there is a question mark or concern about a student, then a referral should be made to a person trained in risk assessment. Teachers are also advised to have a sensitive, but direct and open, discussion with the student in question. In the case of a student who has been reported to be talking about suicide, teachers should ask them directly whether they are thinking of killing themselves; this will give the student the opportunity to talk openly about their feelings.

In the case of a student confirming that he/she has been thinking of taking his/her life, teachers are advised to assess the level of risk by finding out if the student has attempted suicide before and whether or not there are family difficulties such as parental separation, recent bereavement, serious illness etc. Teachers are also advised to ask about personal difficulties the student may have experienced on either a physical or emotional level – these difficulties could include recent hospitalisation, chronic illness, depression, loneliness, guilt or anger. Two other very important questions to determine the immediacy of the risk are whether the student has a plan in place to take his/her life – this could include having written suicide notes, set a date and established means. The more *yes* answers to the above questions, the greater the need for onward referral of the student. Schools are advised that parents should be informed immediately and asked to bring their child to their GP or another service.

Mrs Smith says that both parents and teachers need to be on the lookout for students who are at risk. The school now provides parenting courses. The parents of first years, in particular, benefit from learning about the trends and challenges facing their children in modern Ireland and are advised on the best ways of coping. Teachers are professionally trained and will often pick up on signs that something is not right. 'Often, huge learning difficulties and under-achievement are a sign of pressures and worries, as is irregular attendance.' The problems the students are facing could be anything from family split-ups, disharmony in the home, to peer-group pressure, which Mrs Smith says is more serious than we realise. 'Teachers go beyond the remit of teaching in Irish society. Although we have a full-time school counsellor, often an individual teacher will act as a counsellor as well.' Teachers working with students outside the classroom at games, school concerts etc. may be given a glimpse of a problem not always evident in the ordinary classroom setting.

Mrs Smith says that suicide is an issue that schools need to be prepared for – both in terms of identifying students who may be at risk and in terms of supporting students in the unlikely event of a tragedy. She says that it sometimes occurs (though it is uncommon) that students come to her to tell her of their concerns about other students who may have attempted suicide or have talked about ending their lives. 'Schools have to have a plan in place to deal with this serious problem. Students who come to me or other teachers to express their fears for a friend need to be treated with the utmost of trust. They are under a lot of peer pressure not to "rat" on their friends and the fact that they approach a member of staff highlights their very genuine and heartfelt concern.'

'We treat incidents like these in total confidence. Our first step is to contact the parents of the student we have been told is at risk and let parents know of services in the school and outside the school that are available. Then, with the parents' permission, we would contact the Health Board and inform them that we believe the student has attempted suicide. They would give us various items of advice and we would advise the parents. With the permission of the student who came to us, we contact that individual's parents as well. We take them into confidence, they have to be able to trust us.'

The NEPS points out in its information pack that, in the event of an actual suicide occurring, specific actions must be taken to minimise the emotional trauma that will face other students. The death of a student is a terrible tragedy for any school, all the more so if it is a death by suicide. While very few schools will experience such a major crisis, most schools, at some time or another, experience traumatic situations such as the sudden death of a student or teacher. The effect of the loss of a fellow student or teacher on other students, especially when it is a suicide, is particularly traumatic. In their formative years, students look to teachers and other adults in the school environment to ensure their safety and security. The death of one of their contemporaries is frightening and shakes their sense of security as they realise that their school world is not such a safe haven, completely free from tragedy. In times of such heartbreak, students need reassurance and support from the adults around them as they are confronted with the cold reality of loss and the associated bewilderment and pain.

While there has not been a student suicide in the school where Mrs Smith is principal, the suicide of a friend of two of the school's students had a traumatic effect on many students in the school. A transition year student in a school nearby took his life, but before doing so sent text messages to two girls in Mrs Smith's school, telling them what he was going to do. 'It upset them tremendously. One of the girl's parents contacted me as their daughter was not in school and told me what happened. The word filtered through the school and parents started to call to find out what was going on. The school had to take immediate action to provide support for the girls through the school counsellor and to recommend outside services.'

Mrs Smith says that the effect of such a loss on young students is highly traumatic. 'The problem is so strong in their minds. Students can be disturbed and deeply traumatised – they are crying out for help. You can't carry that trauma yourself. It's a community thing and you have to be very careful and treat the students with the utmost of sensitivity. It is very important to work closely with parents and provide support to them as even parents can have difficulties in coping with problems like these.'

A designated member of staff made contact with the girls in question and the counsellor, together with the school, decided on how to approach talking with the whole class. In such situations, a special staff meeting is called and people are brought in from outside. 'We would organise for these professionals to talk to the parents of the class in question. It is also essential to talk to parents who have heard word of the situation on the street and tell them what has happened and what the school is doing to solve the problem. It is important to be honest and straight with parents.'

Situations such as these are bewildering for students throughout the school because the foundations of their security are shaken and they wonder why such a tragedy is happening. 'There is a chain reaction. An incident like this is huge and it does affect everybody, even students outside that immediate group. Students will worry about it and carry the problem around with them. It affects all students and we have to provide a forum where they can discuss the problem and show them that suicide is not the way – that there is plenty of support for them out there and tell them where they can go to get it, either within the school or outside. Religion class can be especially useful and problems can be aired in front of the teacher, a professional person, who can guide the class in a very careful, professional way.' Mrs Smith says not everyone will air their problems and, by and large, girls are much more inclined to do so than boys. 'They will bring up questions about suicide and the issue can be dealt with.'

The Department of Education and Science has recognised the particular trauma that permeates the school environment in the event of a suicide or similar tragedy. Through the NEPS, they have produced *Responding to Critical Incidents: Advice and Information Pack for Schools* in order to help them to cope with such incidents. The pack provides practical, step-by-step guidelines for teachers and principals on how to respond when a tragedy occurs.

In the foreword to the resource pack, the then Minister for Education asserted that the number of critical incidents experienced by schools appears to have increased in recent years. In his opinion, forward planning is the key to managing such critical incidents. The NEPS advises schools to develop a Critical Incident Management Plan in readiness for any such event and to have a Critical Incident Management Team in place. A meeting of this team can then be called immediately and will facilitate a co-ordinated response. An immediate staff meeting is recommended in order to brief staff on the facts and to prepare teachers and other staff to break the news to students.

The NEPS advises against the use of the term 'suicide' until it is 'established categorically that the student's or teacher's death was as a result of suicide' (ASTI guidelines, 1997).

It is suggested that contact be made with the family in question in order to establish the facts and determine the family's wishes as to how the death should be described. The NEPS advises that two members of school staff should visit the family at home. In order to minimise hurt and confusion and to provide appropriate support, the family should be consulted about the role of the school in the organisation of the funeral service. School management, together with the critical incident management team or pastoral team, should decide who will be visiting the family.

As the experience will be traumatic for many students, staff are advised by the NEPS to identify high-risk students and to inform teachers of supports that are available *(Responding to Critical Incidents: Advice and Information Pack for Schools)*. Those students at high risk will include:

- Close friends and relatives of the deceased
- Pupils with a history of suicide attempts/self-harm
- Pupils who experienced a recent loss, death of a friend or relative, family divorce or separation, break-up with a boyfriend/girlfriend
- Pupils who have been bereaved by a suicide in the past
- Pupils with a psychiatric history
- Pupils with a history of substance abuse
- Pupils with a history of sexual abuse
- Non-communicative students who have difficulty talking about their feelings
- Pupils experiencing serious family difficulties, including serious mental or physical illness
- Less able students

(Mrs Smith is not the school principal's real name. Her name has been changed to protect the anonymity of the people concerned.)

Improving the Inquest Process

A number of families who have been bereaved by suicide have had their trauma prolonged and intensified as a result of the inquest that followed. Families report attending the inquest of their loved one and being forced to sit through the horrific details of other suicides, and sometimes those of road traffic accidents and homicides as well. What some families find particularly upsetting is the courtroom setting of the inquest: they have to take the stand and give evidence, despite the fact that suicide is not a crime. In some cases, inquests have been so badly organised that the family has missed their loved one's inquest and are still left wondering about a lot of the details surrounding the person's death (see Chapter 9).

It should also be remembered that most bereaved families are not familiar with the inquest process or even with court procedures, so they simply do what they are told to do. If they are told to turn up, they turn up, but if they don't receive notification, then they may miss the inquest.

There can be added complications in the case of inquests at which the evidence given and the conclusions drawn may have a bearing on future criminal proceedings; in such cases, the family may need to have a solicitor there to keep 'a watching brief' on the proceedings.

Sr Sheila O'Kelly of the Support Group for the Suicide Bereaved in Bray, Co. Wicklow, says that some of the bereaved people who have come to her for support have had to wait 9–12 months for an inquest, which means they can't even begin to move on with their lives.

Many families find themselves stuck in a legal limbo, unable to attend to pressing practical and legal matters until the inquest process has been completed. Waiting for an inquest to happen can place undue hardship on those already struggling to cope with their grief. There is also the sadness of waiting, the lack of closure and the feeling that their lives cannot move on until after the inquest.

The actual organisation of the inquest can also make things very difficult for the family, held as it has to be, in an open courtroom or, in the case of larger cities, in a specialist coronor's court. This means that there is no privacy for the bereaved family; their most personal information is open to the public and, of course, the media.

I have spoken to a journalist who believes that these cases should not be open to everyone or that reporting should, at least, be restricted. She cites one example of a suicide note being produced in court and promptly reproduced in a newspaper. Undoubtedly, some reporters are sensitive to the families concerned, but others are just looking for a sensationalist headline.

Sr Sheila is particularly angry about the fact that anyone can wander in off the street and listen to the details of a bereaved person's highly personal trauma. She says that the sometimes uncaring nature of the inquest process must change. 'In some courts where inquests are held, you're just a number. Sometimes people have to travel from hundreds of miles away for the inquest and they don't even get a cup of tea.' Sr Sheila wrote to a number of government ministers requesting the provision of basic facilities for the bereaved in the vicinity of the Coroner's Court, so that they could be a little more comfortable while dealing with their grief. 'If we could just get the facilities to offer a cup of tea in the Coroner's Court – just a room.' Sr Sheila believes that the 1962 Coroners' Act badly needs updating.

County Louth Coroner Ronan Maguire B.L. agrees that the 1962 Coroners' Act is an archaic piece of legislation. Legally, he says, a jury is not actually necessary for an inquest in the case of suicide. 'Some coroners will sit for a day and will sit for a jury in every case. I think it's unnecessary. A jury comprises a minimum of six people, which, I believe, is six people too many.' At the 2006 Coroners' Conference, it was proposed that moot inquests should be introduced in order to establish best practice guidelines for all inquests. Maguire hopes that this will result in inquests into suicide being less traumatic for bereaved families.

He says that sometimes suicide inquests are not handled properly and tells me of the case of a man who lost his son to suicide and who rang up a national radio show to talk about the inquest. The bereaved father had to sit through 10 other inquests before his own came up. 'A lot of people are trying very hard to change this structure, but a coroner who has been there for the past 30 years is used to this format. They hold all of the inquests on one day, every one or two months, and have a jury sit for every case.'

Maguire strives to make inquests in the case of suicide as bearable as possible in Co. Louth. Providing families with a running order in advance means that they know exactly what time they have to attend the court and don't need to sit through other cases; it also means that other people don't sit through theirs. 'The last thing you want is to hear everybody else's cases and suffer the pain of listening to other people's tragedies.' Maguire says that the only people whose attendance at the inquest is necessary are the coroner, the Garda, the inspector, the pathologist and the family. To reduce the intimidation of a courtroom setting, Maguire uses the more modern courts rather than the rooms with the big, high chairs and he does not have a jury. At the time of speaking to Maguire, he told me that the law was actually changing and that juries were set to be abolished in the case of suicide inquests.

Although it is necessary for evidence to be given, Maguire makes an effort to create a dialogue, so that the family is not intimidated by a cold, impersonal process. 'We sit around together and the typical duration is 20 minutes.' Before the pathologist goes through the report, Maguire asks whether they need to read the full report out or whether a summary will do. Sometimes, every line has to be heard. While some coroners will actually read out the full contents of a suicide note at an inquest, Maguire believes this is an added and unnecessary ordeal for the bereaved persons. 'I would never ever read out a suicide note. We just state that a suicide note is in existence. It shouldn't be read out.' If the family is not there, Maguire believes in adjourning the inquest immediately, unless they have indicated their intention not to be present.

While there are many advocates for introducing the system that is in place in Northern Ireland, where it lies at the discretion of the coroner whether they want to hold an inquest, Maguire believes the inquest should remain mandatory in the Republic. 'The inquest is an important step for the families.'

An inquest is called for any death that is unnatural, as in the case of suicide, road traffic accidents, homicides or when the cause of death is unknown. The statutory requirement is that coroners must view the body, unless the Gardaí already have; in practice, the Gardaí always view the body. The Gardaí act as coroners. A body will only be brought in for DNA testing or to assess dental records if it is unidentifiable. Maguire says there are rarely problems in terms of identification in instances of suicide, but he says the verdict of suicide is quite a difficult one to call as there has to be satisfaction that it is suicide beyond reasonable doubt. In certain cases, where it is not clear that a person has died by suicide, such as with drownings, the coroner cannot assume it was suicide without the presence of a note. About one-third of people who die by suicide leave notes. A verdict of suicide is a lot more clear-cut in the case of hanging or shooting.

'In Drogheda, there are a huge number of drownings and everybody presumes they are a suicide. If there is no note and nobody saw the person going in, there is no proof. Did they jump? Were they pushed? Did they slip?' Maguire says drownings and drink overdoses are quite difficult to call as suicides unless the individual has expressed intention; often a verdict of accidental death is called instead. In some cases, such as in a drowning, people often presume it was a suicide, but, without proof, in law, it cannot be recorded as a suicide. Maguire believes that under natural justice families are entitled to make a representation. When it is not clear whether a drowning was accidental or the result of suicide, an open verdict is recorded with the medical cause of death. While there have been numerous reports in the media of single car road traffic accidents being possible suicides, Maguire says that a very small proportion of them are likely to be suicides. 'If I was asked, I would say in nine years, just two of all the road traffic accidents I have dealt with were possibly suicides, but you never know. There was no concrete evidence or suicide notes.'

Maguire says that some coroners in Ireland still do not report suicide verdicts: owing to the stigma and criminality that surrounded suicide in the past, they are very reluctant to bring a verdict of suicide, especially if they have been in the job for a number of decades. There is a perception among some people that, for insurance reasons, families do not want suicide recorded as a verdict. However, Maguire says, most policies usually have a trigger of just one year.

These instances should not, however, lead to the statistical under-reporting of suicide as the Gardaí also make a confidential return to the Central Statistics Office, in which they offer their professional opinion as to whether the death in question was a suicide or not. The North Eastern Health Board also work with the coroner, going through his files and asking him to identify possible and definite suicides. Maguire says that most families will agree with the coronor if he is considering a verdict of suicide. 'The law is the law. You can't twist the law.'

Up until 1993, suicide was a crime in Ireland. Under the 1962 Coroners' Act, if a verdict of suicide was recorded, it implied that the deceased had committed a crime. As a result, the courts were very reluctant to record a verdict of suicide and verdicts of suicide were quashed. The 1962 Coroners' Act also states that a verdict of death can never contain a statement of criminal or civil liability on behalf of any person named on the death certificate. This, says Maguire, would have had a big effect on the rates of suicide reported. 'In the old days, even the Gardaí would have been reluctant to suggest suicide (even confidentially), principally because of the idea of it being a crime. It's so surreal – what are they going to do to the person!'

With the decriminalisation of suicide in 1993, Maguire says that, in theory, suicide verdicts were made possible, but the stigma and the idea of suicide being a crime lingered, even in official circles. 'There was a case in Co. Galway, where the jury's verdict was "discharge of a rifle while the balance of the mind was disturbed" rather than suicide. The case was appealed to the Supreme Court and it was decided in the Supreme Court that how death occurs is to be determined in the light of medical science, so quite a lot of deaths were recorded in accordance with the medical evidence, such as "asphyxiation due to hanging", with no underlying verdict of suicide.' This suceeded in limiting the scope of inquests for a while.

Maguire, along with other coroners throughout the country, decided to bring in verdicts of suicide and then in 2003, draft coroners' rules brought suicide in as a proper verdict. A verdict of suicide now reads 'asphyxiation due to hanging, due to suicide'. Though there is a perception that death by misadventure can apply in the case of suicide, Maguire says that death by misadventure refers to the unintentional consequence of an intentional action and applies, for example, when someone is intoxicated and goes for a swim and drowns. Intoxication is the cause of the drowning, but the person did not set out to drown.

In his nine years as County Coroner for Louth, Ronan Maguire has dealt with approximately 100 suicides. Reflecting national statistics, he says that the majority of the people were in their twenties and young males, though female suicides were on the increase at the time (2005) and female suicides were also starting to become more violent.

He noted that suicide rates were particularly high at Christmas time and the New Year and also observed that 44–46 per cent of the suicides he dealt with involved alcohol. 'There is alcohol in the person's system in a lot of cases. You can get an exact reading and tell from the correlation between blood and urine when it was consumed.'

'The Boyne River in Drogheda goes straight through the town. People come out of the pubs and clubs with huge levels of alcohol and end up in the river. On some occasions they jump in.' One guideline for suicide prevention is to remove the means by which a person can take their lives – clearly, in the case of a river, this is virtually impossible. In the case of the River Foyle, which flows through Derry City (see chapter 16), volunteers physically prevent people from throwing themselves into the river at high-risk times (Thursday, Friday and Saturday nights).

I asked Maguire if there was anything that could be done to speed up the inquest process, thereby easing the suffering of families who are trying to find closure. Unfortunately, however, with suicide, the process is not simple. The time-frame from death to inquest is complicated in the case of suicide. In almost all suicides, blood and urine samples are taken. These samples can provide a measurement of the quantity of alcohol in the blood, but if there are other substances in the person's system, the process can be delayed by six to nine months before the results come in. 'In many overdose cases, it will take three to four months minimum for the results to come in from the state laboratory.' Still, suicide cases tend to come to inquest sooner than homicide cases as there is usually no Garda investigation into suicide.

The inquest process in the case of homicides is often much more drawn out. The coroner can only open the inquest and evidence of identification is presented. Often, the Gardaí will ask for the case to be adjourned on the basis that someone is to be charged or exonerated, as it wouldn't make sense to proceed with the inquest prior to an investigation. There can also be considerable delays with road traffic accidents when there is liability.

Another issue that bereaved families raise is the difficulty of sorting out the financial affairs of the deceased person if there is a delay with the inquest. Maguire says an interim death certificate is accepted by quite a lot of banks and financial institutions when an inquest is dragging on and coroners' rules say that they should be accepted. Another issue for some families is the fact that the death certificate that they have to use for all official business states that the individual died by suicide and this can be seen by whoever they are dealing with. Maguire says there is very little that can be done about this as the death certificate is a legal document. 'It's a matter of public record. It's there in black and white. You can't start fiddling around with facts.'

Suicide and the Church

The stigma surrounding suicide dates back to the time of St Augustine, who in the early fifth century wrote his arguments opposing suicide. Although the Bible itself does not specifically condemn suicide, Augustine pointed to the sixth commandment – 'Thou Shalt Not Kill' – to support his argument. From the perspective of the state, it was a crime until 1993 and from the point of view of the Catholic Church, it was regarded as a grave sin, which denied the person burial in consecrated ground.

Fr Aidan Troy of Holy Cross Parish says the pastoral approach to suicide varies among individual priests, which has helped to change the outlook of the church. Indeed, attitudes have become a lot more sympathetic and nowadays very few priests will refuse to bury a person who has died by suicide in consecrated ground. No-one in Ireland has been refused burial in consecrated ground since 1950.

Catholic priest, Rev. Dr Tony Byrne, insists that anybody worried that their loved ones who have died by suicide are going to hell has to get that out of their minds as no-one who takes their own life can be held responsible. 'For serious sin, you would need full consent and full knowledge.'

In terms of the issue of burial in consecrated ground, Rev. Dr Byrne explains that Canon 1240, which denied Christian burial to 'persons guilty of suicide', has been removed from Church Law and Christian burial for suicides is permitted by all of the Christian churches today. Rev. Dr Tony Byrne advises against using the term 'commit suicide' as this indicates that the deceased has committed a crime. He says that describing it as 'loss by suicide or death by suicide' is better; otherwise, grieving people will feel that their loved ones are criminals and have gone to hell. 'Be careful about hurting people and causing pain by the terminology used,' he says.

From his extensive work in the area of suicide, he observes that people who kill themselves are usually very good people, people who have done a lot to enrich the lives of their families and communities. 'They didn't want to die, but they felt they couldn't live.'

In a paper on Suicide and the Church, Sr Sheila O'Kelly of the Support Group for the Suicide Bereaved in Bray, Co. Wicklow, is adamant that suicide is not a mortal sin. 'It's a totally irrational act.' Under the catechism so familiar to earlier generations, she says a mortal sin is defined as composing the following three elements: a grave matter, full knowledge and full consent.

Death is a grave matter; however, she says that the existence of full knowledge is very doubtful, considering that before a person dies by suicide the blinds have already been drawn over the protective windows of that person's mind. The existence of full consent in the mind of a suicidal person is the most doubtful. The decisions people make and the actions they undertake when they are depressed or their mind is clouded by alcohol or drugs are rarely rational.

'If the person's action is to be judged a sin, we are asserting the belief that he demonstrated at the time full knowledge and full consent. It is both just and appropriate hence that they are given the dignity and the full benefits of a Christian burial in consecrated ground. It is noteworthy that the churches have been doing this long before civil decriminalisation was put in place in 1993.'

However, there are still some members of the Catholic Church in Ireland (albeit a tiny minority) who view suicide as an act against God, as opposed to the action of a desperate individual. Some of the stories in this book show the tremendous pain that can be caused to bereaved families when a member of the Church speaks in a condemnatory manner about the person who has died by suicide.

In the majority of cases, however, bereaved families have received tremendous support from members of the Catholic Church. In the course of my research, I frequently met with Catholic priests and nuns who run support groups for families bereaved by suicide and who have dedicated themselves to assisting people who feel desperate enough to take their lives. Sr Sheila O'Kelly says that the blame does not lie with the person who takes their lives and describes these individuals as victims.

'The churches have a duty to face openly, in words and deeds, the reality of life in Ireland. We must confront the loneliness of modern life. Very often, the victims of suicide are among the most innocent and vulnerable of people. Somewhere, in that lonely ground between condemnation and romanticism, there lies a human story where the Cross of Christ is planted. Hope lies in our finding that place and opening out the truth to those who stand by the cross uncomprehending.'

Fr Aidan Troy of Holy Cross Parish, Ardoyne, Belfast, explains that, historically, the Catholic Church interpreted suicide as an individual playing God. '"God gives life and only God can take it back" lies at the heart of the argument.' Fr Troy says that another moral objection was that the person who takes their own life is failing in love towards themselves, as they are taking away the possibility of growing and developing. 'Basically, because the person had acted against God and failed in their life's vocation, the Church placed them literally outside the bounds of the church and buried them in unconsecrated ground.' Fr Troy says that this practice and thinking was international and not just specific to Ireland. The American Catholic Encyclopaedia of 1912 basically confirms what Fr Troy has said above.

'The best source of the thinking of the Catholic Church is the catechism published some years ago by the Vatican. In essence, you can see that the role of psychological insight has helped moralists and teachers to appreciate that suicide is not just a rational decision taken in a cool and calculating manner.'

Similarly, a more sympathetic attitude has developed in the Church of Ireland. In 2005, I spoke to the Bishop of Cork, the Right Reverend Paul Colton, who told me that attitudes would be tested at the General Synod the following year [2006], when he planned to propose a bill which would remove the discretionary right clergy had not to read the burial office at the burial of those who have suicided. He said that for many years, there had been a reference to that discretionary right in the Book of Common Prayer.

Fr Pat O'Donoghue, Director of the Dublin Diocesan Liturgical Resource Centre, re-evaluated the liturgy for the suicide bereaved in an article in *Intercom* in May 1999. He altered his liturgy after showing a draft to someone who had attempted to take her own life. She had no issue with the first two sections on remembrance of those who had taken their own lives and providing comfort and consolation to their family and friends. It was the third part of the liturgy that she had a problem with, the section that set out to 'offer light of hope to those who might consider suicide'. The girl felt that the 'leap from desperation to hope had been nothing short of pantomime magic'. Although it had not been the intention, the girl felt that the message was 'as if we could implant hope and make everything better'. Fr O'Donoghue says that this highlighted the need for sensitivity when preparing such a liturgy and has now revised his position: 'Before moving to any consideration of hope, we must first try to identify with the darkness of depression and despair.'

Religious faith is actually recognised as a significant protective factor against suicide. The huge rise in Irish suicide rates has seen a parallel decline in the role of religion. The diminishing position of the Catholic Church, though not considered a causal factor of suicide, is part of a complex mixture of factors that have arisen as a result of major changes in society. In his book *Suicide Awareness*, President of the Irish Association of Suicidology (IAS), Dan Neville TD, points to factors in other countries which have been found to correlate highly with the suicide rate. These include the 'increase in indictable crime, the increase in alcoholism, the increase in birth rates to single mothers and the rate of marriage breakdown', all of which are represented in modern Irish society. Neville explains that none of these factors offer a causative explanation, 'but suggests that the same forces that lead to these changes are also influencing the rates of suicide'.

Neville also refers to the wane in traditional religious values, particularly among the young. In Irish society in the past, religion provided community structures as well as social controls. The drop in faith has taken away a lot of what was once a certainty in society. Neville points out that the growing secularisation of society has changed the value system. 'Social controls are less strict and often people feel alone and lost. There is no longer a prearranged set of relationships, with certainty within the relationship, as was the case in past generations.'

The fact that women are traditionally more involved in religion than men is noted as a factor that may also contribute to the lower rate of suicide among women. In Ireland, the rate of suicide in younger women is on the increase, against a background of a decline in religious faith.

Dr Patricia Casey, Professor of Psychiatry in the Mater Hospital/UCD refers to Durkheim's work, in which he says that countries that had the lowest suicide rates were countries where religious belief strongly condemned suicide, while the opposite applied in those that were not similarly judgemental. 'The protective values of religious belief seem to be related to the extent to which these are part.'

Casey suggests that there are several routes by which religious beliefs could protect against suicide. 'Firstly, having strongly held beliefs about the sacredness of life can act as a break against suicidal thoughts, impulses and behaviour. Also, it is recognised that religious beliefs act as a counterweight to some risk factors for depression, the illness most clearly associated with suicide. Moreover, those of a religious persuasion have a circle of friends from their church and associated organisations that offer support at times of crisis when people are vulnerable to suicidal thoughts; although this has been shown in most studies to be less important than the belief system itself.' This highlights the way in which those with strong involvement with religion can be better integrated into society.

In 2004, the Irish Catholic bishops addressed the problem of suicide in Ireland through a newsletter entitled *Life is for Living. A*

Reflection on Suicide. As part of the 'Day for Life' 2004, they set out to explore the issue and offer support 'in the hope that those who may think of suicide would reconsider their situation and those who have been bereaved through self-inflicted deaths may, eventually, with God's help, begin to understand what has happened and find peace'.

The newsletter points to the weakening of faith which accompanied the arrival of economic success to this country and, while the Catholic bishops describe the desire to reduce the stigma around suicide in the past as 'laudable', they point out that this has resulted in 'the erosion of the recognition that suicide is an unthinkable option'. While the desire is not to return to the condemnatory status of old or to return to the severe stigma, the Catholic bishops say that, as a society, we must recognize the 'terrifying reality' of suicide and together acknowledge and confront it. 'In particular, we need to recognise the danger that resignation to the idea that there is little we can do to prevent suicide could develop in our society.'

The newsletter presents the belief of the Catholic Church that life is for living and God's gift, hence only God can decide when life ends. Still, they do not use the newsletter as a means to condemn suicide outright, rather it aims to help individuals cope with the difficulties life presents and offers support and hope that it doesn't have to be like that. They recognise that throughout the world, people are faced with challenges and difficulties, but point out that, 'The fact remains that, no matter how great the suffering, the darkness passes eventually. Our faith assures us that if we turn to God in our loneliness and pain then we can discover that our darkness is not something created by God. It is a reality from which God wants to rescue us and through which we can triumph.'

The Catholic bishops suggest that advertising can be misleading and contribute to a promise that there are easy and instant solutions to almost everything in life, when in reality this is not the case. The newsletter calls on everyone, particularly Ireland's youth, to hold on 'and then go on to discover the wonder of life and living'.

The newsletter further reiterates the message of professionals, that communication is essential. 'It is good to talk and it is important to talk. Men, in particular, seem to be poor when it comes to talking out problems, but we all need to remember that expression is the conqueror of depression.' The newsletter represents the more sympathetic attitude of the Catholic Church to the problem of suicide. It does not blast suicide as a mortal sin, but reminds us that suicide is not a solution and, in terms of the Catholic Church, individuals should not play God. In contrast to messages of eternal damnation from the Church in the past, the newsletter offers an understanding, rather than a condemnatory, approach. 'While we believe that "God is the giver of life, and he alone has the right to decide when that life should end", we also realise that God can look deep within the human heart, recognise its difficulties, understand and forgive. We should always pray for those who take their own lives, try to understand them and commend them to God's mercy.'

The newsletter reflects the view of the IAS and other experts, including voluntary organisations, that suicide prevention is everyone's responsibility and concludes by appealing to everyone to work together. 'We call on everyone, individuals, families, schools, colleges, communities, the government, the media and health care systems to join in the effort to make the causes of suicide more fully understood, the care of those at risk more urgent and the families of those bereaved by suicide consoled and supported, so that everyone in our country will feel cherished and cared for, especially in these tragic circumstances. In particular, we encourage and support the development of suicide prevention strategies.'

Mary: Coming Through the Pain

Accident and Emergency is confronted with 10,000 attempted suicides – parasuicides – in Ireland every year, and these are just the reported parasuicides. Experts estimate that a further 40,000 parasuicides may go unreported in Ireland every year. Over the course of my research for this book, I met with a number of individuals who had attempted to take their lives in the past, but fortunately were unsuccessful in their attempts.

Among those I spoke to, many were in counselling and working on their problems, many were worlds beyond the desperation they had once felt and many reported that thoughts of suicide seemed alien to the person they had become. The number of individuals who have succeeded in seeking help for their problems and who have learned to cope (to the extent of becoming professional counsellors themselves or extremely successful in other areas) was very encouraging and gave true meaning to the description of suicide as a 'permanent solution to a temporary problem'.

Below is the story of Mary, who attempted to take her life on numerous occasions but, after a long struggle to identify and treat the root cause of her problems, has come through the other side and is now heavily involved in trying to prevent suicide in Ireland. As with all of the stories in this book, it is worth recalling that people who are suicidal are not in the same rational frame of mind as others and Mary's honest and open account of her experience offers the opportunity to try to understand. It also offers an insight into what it can be like to feel so low, desperate and hopeless that life does not seem worth living, whilst also showing that feelings such as these do not need to last forever, that there is help out there.

Mary had a breakdown when she was just 16 years of age. On an evening out with her boyfriend, she suddenly had to leave the restaurant as a result of excruciating stomach pains. She rushed home in a taxi and from there went straight to hospital. The verdict was that she was having a nervous breakdown.

She was put on different types of medication, including valium and anti-depressants, but no indication was given as to what was causing her problems. She was unwilling to stay at the hospital and went for treatment as an out-patient instead. Over the following months, Mary began to feel much happier, on a high, even. Looking back, however, she realises that she wasn't getting better; instead, the medication was numbing the pain. 'I was going around in a stupor.'

Things got progressively worse in Mary's life. She left school around this time: 'I hated school.' Coming from an affluent family, Mary was not particularly liked by her peers in a school where her contemporaries were less well-off than she was. She did get a good job as a supervisor in a telecommunications company, but was unable to hold it down. The heavy medication was taking its toll and over the next few years she drifted from job to job. Something was clearly not right, but Mary was unable to identify what it was. She didn't realise that there were underlying causes of the pain she was experiencing.

She had very little support around her. Her boyfriend since she was 12 was her only friend and, though he made an effort, Mary could see that he didn't really understand what she was going through. Her parents wouldn't accept that she had a problem. As far as they were concerned, a problem connected with mental illness was a taboo problem to have. Her father and her brother kept telling her to snap out of it and concentrate on her studies, so Mary began to wonder whether they might just be right and she stopped going to the hospital for treatment. However, things continued to get worse and very soon Mary went back to hospital again, where she received counselling.

Once again she would only attend as an out-patient. In counselling, she recalls feeling incredibly uncomfortable when she was asked about the physical side of her relationship with her boyfriend. In actual fact, there was no physical side, but for some reason Mary felt so ill at ease discussing it that she wouldn't go back to the hospital again. Her anti-depressant medication continued and though it seemed to stop her from getting any worse, it wasn't making her any better. She was in her own little world all the time. 'I didn't know anyone around me who had this problem. I didn't understand what it was.'

Work was a disaster as Mary continued on medication. She couldn't settle at anything and found she was blaming everyone else – her supervisor, other members of staff. She was continuously feeling on a low.

When Mary was 22, she broke up with her boyfriend of more than 9 years and went over to the Isle of Man to help her sister, who was going through a divorce at the time. It was on the Isle of Man that she first met Michael, an older 'man of the world', who instantly swept her off her feet. When Mary's sister moved to the UK, Mary went too and began a relationship with Michael, a divorcee.

Things seemed to be going well until Mary found out that Michael was actually still living with his wife and it turned out that he also had children. Mary was devastated and overnight her world fell to pieces. Her immediate reaction was to visit Michael's wife and apologise for any hurt she may have caused. Michael's wife was very understanding and kind, realising that Mary hadn't known that he was still married. There was nothing to keep Mary in England any more, so she returned to Ireland to try and put her life back together.

However, it wasn't long before Michael followed her over and threatened to tell her parents about their relationship if she didn't come back to England with him. Knowing that her conservative parents would disown her if they knew about the relationship, Mary agreed to go back. She knew that if her parents found out about Michael and his children, it would confirm all of the negative opinions they had about her. Michael had got a legal separation from his wife and wanted Mary to move in with him back in the UK, and she did. She stopped taking her medication around this time and was able to discuss the problems she was experiencing with Michael, who seemed to understand. 'Michael took care of me. He was a gentleman, a man of the world and I was in awe of him.'

Still, Mary constantly felt low. She worked on and off as a temp while she was with Michael, but was plagued by feelings of fear and isolation. She didn't have many other friends to talk to or turn to for support. 'I felt that I wanted to die.'

Things reached crisis point one day when Michael was visiting his children. Mary was on her own and she started to get a headache. She started crying and that only made the headache worse. The worse the headache got, the more she cried and finally emotional pain she could not explain or understand took over. The pain was so excruciating that she felt she didn't want to go on and, in that moment, she tried to kill herself.

She woke up in a hospital bed, surrounded by doctors. All she felt was blackness in her head; she didn't want them to save her – she just didn't care anymore. 'I felt there was nothing there for me – I was alone.' Still, Mary recovered from her suicide attempt and was released from the hospital, to return soon after as an in-patient. The mental anguish was still unbearable, however, and Mary was not recovering. She still felt that she didn't want to go on. Then, Michael came to visit her and took her out in the car for the day. 'I just felt like I didn't want to be here. All I wanted was out.' She jumped from the moving car, trying again to end it all. Amazingly, however, she wasn't even hurt and Michael brought her back to the hospital.

Mary remained in the hospital as an in-patient for a number of months and when it seemed she was much better, she was discharged on the condition that she avail of the outreach service. In reality, however, things weren't getting any better. Mary felt desperately low and at a loss to understand what was making her feel that way. Following another attempt, Mary was taken back into hospital and stayed there for a further three months, after which she moved to Surrey, where friends had organised a nice place for her to rent. She was on medication and had to visit her doctor on a daily basis. During this period, Mary started to improve significantly. Her doctor was very kind to her and after ten months, she felt ready to return to Ireland.

Shortly after her return home, Mary met her future husband. She was about 26 at the time. Straight away, Mary was able to be very open with him and told him everything about her relationship with Michael in England. The two had their first child together and Mary was thrilled. Though her relationship with her daughter was fine, the birth had unearthed something deep inside that caused a problem in her relationship with her husband; the physical side of their relationship deteriorated. Mary did not want her husband to touch her, and had no understanding of what was causing this.

Still, life continued and soon Mary got pregnant again. She faced further trauma when she lost her second baby four and a half months into the pregnancy. The birth of her next child was very difficult and she remembers the midwife removing the afterbirth manually. 'I went ballistic.' The traumatic events were taking their toll and suddenly Mary's former problems began to resurface. 'I woke up feeling nothing. I went to counselling, but left as soon as I started to feel okay again.'

Mary continued to go back and forth to counselling but the underlying cause of a lot of the trauma that she had experienced throughout her life only became clear some years later. The birth of her first child had unearthed feelings about something from her past, which she would discover was one of the serious underlying causes of the emotional issues she had had since she was in her teens.

Mary discovered that she had been sexually abused by her father when she was a child. She had blocked the ordeal from her memory for all those years, but it had had a profound effect on her life, nonetheless. Mary's GP sent her to counselling and finally she could begin to deal with this harrowing experience that lay at the root of her problems. She had an excellent psychiatrist, complemented by a great counsellor who assisted Mary on the journey to recovery. Mary's father is now dead, but she has learned to forgive him and still visits his grave. 'I loved my father, I still do. For him to do what he did was very sad.'

The underlying cause of Mary's problems was revealed to be traumatic and distressing. Other trials in her life seemed to bring her past experience of abuse to the surface in the form of psychological desperation. A difficult relationship with her mother in her teens hadn't helped matters, either. She recalls how her brothers were the apple of her mother's eye, while she was always the one seeking approval. As an adult, her relationship with her mother changed and the two ended up becoming very close. However, when her mother died, Mary hit rock bottom again. She came very close to ending her life.

'I couldn't sleep … I didn't think about my family … then I did … I remember thinking people die every day of the week and life goes on … I thought the kids will get over it. I didn't want to do it. There were loads of different things going on in my head, it was like stations flicking. I was trying to reason with myself, to give me a reason to stay … it wasn't selfish, it wasn't brave … I didn't exist. I didn't have any feelings inside. I just wanted the pain to stop.'

Mary was on different types of tablets, including sleeping tablets, but she couldn't sleep and would spend entire nights on the phone to the Samaritans. She knew that as long as she was on the phone, she wouldn't do anything. 'Everything came tumbling down around me – the abuse, my mum's death. My self-esteem dropped to an all-time low. I didn't feel I was worth anything. I was someone's mother, someone's daughter, sister, wife and if I took them all out of the equation, I was nothing. I felt I had failed at everything. I had failed as a mother due to my depression.'

Mary just wanted it all to end, even though she knew suicide was a terrible legacy to leave her children. 'I wanted to live, but felt it was the only way to get rid of what was going on in my head. I felt as if my head was going to explode and kept hammering my knuckles against my head.

'People who have severe depression don't think they have a right to exist. Nobody wants to die. They want what's in their head to stop. You need to hang on, hang on in there – it doesn't have to be like this.' On that occasion, with help, Mary did not go as far as she had before and, with professional help, she was able to begin to move through the pain.

'Now I have put a lot of things to bed. I needed to forgive my father for me to go on.' Mary is eternally grateful to the Samaritans who provided the right help when she needed it. She also feels indebted to the counselling service she went to every single day for five years, before reducing her attendance to once a week and eventually attending just group counselling.

Since Mary has learned to let go of the problems from her childhood, her life has changed completely and for the better. 'There's a difference in me. I went back to school. I studied counselling and did my counselling diploma in Maynooth and am now involved in the Drug Rehab Clinic. I'm now going on to study for a degree. Since I've been working on myself, the difference is immense.' Mary will now walk away from situations if they're not good for her. Instead of smothering people and things, as she did in the past, friendships are now formed because she connects with the person. This year, she celebrates her 25th wedding anniversary and she has three fantastic children whom she adores. 'I'm very glad to be alive.'

It may have taken a long time for Mary to deal with the various traumas in her life but she now wants to share the message of hope with everyone who may be feeling as low as she once felt. By sharing her story with others, she wants to communicate that no matter how big or small the problem may be, it doesn't have to be like that. Her message is to keep seeking help. 'Keep asking, you will get it. There is a way out and you can lead a happy and fulfilling life to the point that you're glad to be alive, but first you have to get help.'

Attempted suicide can often be dismissed as attention-seeking and too often people don't take it seriously. One of the common myths associated with attempted suicide is that the person will not really go on to take their lives, despite frequently talking about it. This is a seriously misguided assumption as having made a previous suicide attempt is a powerful predictor of subsequent suicidal behaviour, particularly in the first six months after the attempt.

The figures for attempted suicide among women are significantly higher than those for men, which could appear unusual considering that the suicide rate among men averages at approximately four men for every woman in Ireland. Experts suggest that the fact that men tend to use more violent methods when making an attempt on their lives could be partly responsible for the significant gap between high levels of female attempts and the higher level of actual suicide among males, as opposed to females.

Mary's story is reflective of a very serious problem of attempted suicide that exists in Ireland today. While the 457 deaths by suicide in 2004 raise serious concern, these figures do not reveal the thousands of people who attempt suicide in Ireland every year. Accident and Emergency deal with approximately 10,000 parasuicides in Ireland every year. Parasuicide is defined as 'an act with non-fatal outcome in which an individual deliberately initiates a non-habitual behaviour, that without intervention from others will cause self-harm, or deliberately ingests a substance in excess of the prescribed or generally recognised therapeutic dosage, and which is aimed at realising changes that the person desires via the actual or expected physical consequences' (National Parasuicide Registry). Parasuicide includes acts involving varying levels of suicidal intent, including definite suicide attempts and acts where the individual had little or no intention of dying.

Even more worrying is the professional belief that there are ten parasuicides for every one a GP sees. Secretary of the Irish Association of Suicidology, Dr John Connolly, says that this means that there may be up to 50,000 attempted suicides in Ireland per annum. The 2002 National Parasuicide Registry annual report focused on establishing the extent of the problem of hospital-treated parasuicide in Ireland. It estimated that in 2002 there were approximately 10,500 presentations to hospital due to deliberate self-harm, involving approximately 8,400 individuals.

Despite common misconceptions that attempted suicides are cries for attention and not to be taken seriously, Dan Neville TD in *Suicide Awareness* highlights that people with a history of attempted suicide or self-harm are up to 30 times more at risk of eventually taking their lives than the population average. There is also a serious misconception that if someone has a history of making cries for help, then they won't do it for real. 'The group of people at highest risk for suicide are those who have attempted it in the previous year.' Another serious myth is the notion that the method used in a suicide attempt is indicative of how serious the person is about taking their life. 'Most people have little awareness of the lethality of what they are doing. The seriousness of the attempt is no indication of the seriousness of the intent, except with medical professionals such as doctors and nurses as they know what they're doing from a medical perspective.'

In a 10-year study of suicide among different occupational groups, carried out by Niamh Nic Daéid, vets, doctors, dentists, nurses, pharmacists and chemists were all listed in the top 16 occupations in which suicide levels were over-represented. The study was conducted between 1982 and 1992, during which period the national average for people who died by suicide was eight per 100,000. Vets came in at the top of the specific occupation table with a rate of 34 per 100,000, while dentists were at 32 per 100,000, doctors were 22 per 100,000, pharmacists were 19.6 per 100,000, chemists 12.4 per 100,000 and nurses were 11.4 per 100,000. While clearly these rates do not simply correspond to knowledge of 'how to do it', it is significant that these six specific occupational groups rate so highly. Nic Daéid points out that suicide rates per 100,000 for specific occupational groups may give a distorted view of the actual numbers of suicides in each group. 'The numbers in specific occupations tend to be small, relative to the total population.' There is also the added caveat that all of the professions listed here are easier to measure over a lifetime insofar as it is more likely that, having studied to be a doctor or a dentist, they will stick with their chosen career and not move across different occupations.

Like the actual suicide rate in Ireland, evidence also indicates that the rate of parasuicide in Ireland has increased. The 2002 annual report from the National Parasuicide Registry recorded increases in parasuicide across the four health boards in Ireland, for which a full year's data was collected in 2001. The Midland, Mid-Western, South Eastern and Southern Health Boards experienced increases of 5.7 per cent, 11.9 per cent, 8.5 per cent and 12.7 per cent, respectively, in the rate of individuals presenting to hospital due to parasuicide.

The report found that rates among women are approximately 40 per cent higher than among men – 237 and 167 per 100,000, respectively. Rates are particularly high in the young: currently, 90 per cent of all presentations to hospital as a result of deliberate self-harm involve individuals aged under 50 years of age.

The National Parasuicide Registry is a national system of population monitoring for the occurrence of parasuicide. It has been established, at the request of the Department of Health and Children, by the National Suicide Research Foundation.

Saving Lives along the River Foyle: Searching

Between 1993 and 2005 Foyle Search and Rescue saved 800 individuals from drowning in the Foyle River. From 10 pm to 3 am every Thursday, Friday and Saturday night, a team of three volunteers patrols Craigavon Bridge to prevent people from throwing themselves into the cold waters beneath. These are considered 'high-risk' times. Another team walks up and down the 1.5-mile stretch from the New Foyle Bridge to Craigavon Bridge, while a boat on the river is at the ready if someone does end up in the water. Endless lives have been lost to suicide along this stretch of the river: an average of 35–40 individuals drowned in the river every year prior to the foundation of Foyle Search and Rescue.

Foyle Search and Rescue was founded in 1993. That year, founding organiser Paddy Wilson took part in the search for the body of a local man who had lost his life in the river. A group of concerned people got together and realised that something had to be done to prevent the tragic and extensive loss of life in the River Foyle. They set up the voluntary organisation with the sole aim of preserving human life in and around the River Foyle.

It is striking that the problem of people throwing themselves into the River Foyle, especially on nights when licensed premises were open late, had grown so acute that it was felt that there was a need for volunteers to physically prevent people from entering the waters. I travelled to Derry to spend a Thursday night with the volunteers, out patrolling the banks and the waters of the River Foyle. I hoped to learn more about the reasons why a phenomenal number of people appeared to want to end it all, especially after apparently enjoying themselves on a night out.

When Paddy Wilson brought me into the city centre, I was struck by the proximity of the vast and potentially lethal Foyle River. As alcohol can sometimes have a very negative effect on a person's state of mind and since it increases the risk of dangerous behaviour, a walk that takes just 60 seconds has proven, in the case of the River Foyle, to be life-threatening. At a 2003 IAS conference on alcohol and suicide (Alcohol, Substance Misuse and Suicidal Behaviour), Dr Justin Brophy pointed out that we can sometimes get in touch with our darker forces through the use of alcohol. 'Powerful, destructive influences can arise, a tendency to disagreement and argument, uncovering our baser self, the "demonic" aspects ... ' Although Brophy points out that through alcohol we can 'sense power, skill, strength, freedom, wealth and sexual attractiveness or prowess', he says that, on the other hand, 'we can also experience the anti-heroic possibilities of impotence, uselessness, weakness, failure, recklessness, impoverishment, sexual guilt and rejection in equal measures'. Paddy Wilson says that approximately 95 per cent of the people they come across have taken alcohol, whether it be a little or a lot. The majority of individuals they come across are male and the typical age group is between 18 and 45.

Alcohol per se is not a cause of suicide. When there are other problems present in an individual's mind and an easily accessible means of attempting to take one's life – the River Foyle, for example – the correlation between the various elements, alcohol included, results in a very high number of people attempting to throw themselves in, as has been seen by this group. As relationship break-ups, arguments and social disruption are a fact of everyday life, and the anti-heroic effects of alcohol can lead to arguments and unease, the proximity of the River Foyle to the licensed premises can have fatal results. In fact, one of the ways to reduce suicide is to remove the means of taking one's life, a recourse that is obviously impossible in the case of a river.

Before going out to patrol the river just before 10 pm, we drove through the city. I noted the huge number of people who were out, apparently enjoying themselves, and remembered what Dr John Connolly of the Irish Association of Suicidology (IAS) had said to me about never knowing what goes on in people's heads. He had explained to me how often suicide comes as a complete and utter shock to families, who had believed that their son or daughter was very happy and that their lives were going well. 'People tell their parents what they want to hear. They will never tell them stuff about when they are stupid.' I wondered at all of the young people, full of expectation, out with their friends of a Thursday evening – how many of them would argue with friends that night? How many had just broken up with a boyfriend or girlfriend? How many couldn't get a boyfriend or girlfriend? Were unemployed? Were worried about a problem at home or were in serious debt?

Environmental factors and life events and stresses are listed by the UK National Health Service as risk factors for suicide. High-risk groups include people suffering interpersonal, legal or disciplinary problems, conflict or loss, marital separation or divorce, major exam failure, unwanted pregnancy and those under financial stress. Many of these stresses and events are part of life and if they continue unrecognised and untreated, alcohol may be chosen as a means of drowning one's sorrows. During the evening I spent patrolling the River Foyle, volunteers told me that while a substantial percentage of individuals saved by the organisation appear to be suffering from psychiatric illness, many others have been upset by an argument or a disagreement, which may have only happened that evening or the day before.

Before heading out on patrol, I gathered with the volunteers in the organisation's headquarters, a modern three-storey building on the river bank with a radio control room. Different teams were assigned to cover the river in a lifeboat, to take out the jeep and to walk along the banks in search of troubled individuals thinking about throwing themselves in. I joined the team in the jeep and we were all given high-visibility jackets as it was a dark night.

The evening commenced with a radio check between the jeep and the lifeboat to ensure communication channels were up and running.

Volunteers told me that they would carry out radio checks throughout the evening to make sure that there was no communication failure. The shore patrols are in constant radio contact with the base operator and are the first line of care. Should they observe a person they consider may be in need of help, they make the initial contact. Depending on the situation, they decide whether they need the call-out team, the boat crew or one of the other emergency services. The role of the shore patrol is of crucial importance as they make the initial contact as sensitively as circumstances allow.

The first task of the evening was to carry out a check on all of the life-belts along the river, to make sure they were in place and ready for use in case of emergency. After that it was all about vigilance –the three volunteers and I drove along the banks of the river and over the Craigavon Bridge, a high-risk location for people throwing themselves in, all the while carefully observing for anyone in crisis. As it hit me that we were literally on watch for people who might be trying to take their lives, I was overcome by the gravity of the situation. The volunteers explained to me that the high railings along the Craigavon Bridge had only been erected four years before; prior to that, there were lower railings that were easier to get over. They explained that the smallest thing, such as the height of the railings, can make a significant difference when saving lives, especially as the majority of people trying to climb over have alcohol in their system, making small obstacles more difficult for them to overcome.

The Craigavon Bridge is 40ft high, but even more lethal is the 150ft-high Foyle Bridge. Earlier in the day, Paddy drove me to the bottom of the Foyle Bridge and looking up, I was taken aback by its dizzying height and was suddenly acutely aware of the slim chance of survival for anyone who went over it. The volunteers told me that it is very hard to survive if one falls from that height. We stop the jeep at a key location, giving us a view across the bridge and along the banks of the river. In the distance, we see the light from the lifeboat patrolling the waters. The volunteers notice a girl walking onto the bridge and everyone watches her progress. We lose sight of her for a moment and the jeep's engine is started up. We drive over the bridge and catch sight of her again – she has just reached the other side of the bridge and is on her way home. I realise how seriously this job is taken and reflect on the fact that while we are there, neither that girl nor anyone else will be able to go over the railings without intervention.

Although, thankfully, we didn't come across anyone in crisis that night, the volunteers told me that sometimes they can come across one or two people attempting to throw themselves in on the same night. They said that in such instances they physically do everything in their power to prevent the person from going over the railings. Paddy tells me that the people they come across are rarely happy to see them. 'They want to die and don't want to be saved at that moment in time. They will say things like "Go away! Let me die."' The response of the Foyle Search and Rescue Team is 'We're not going to let you die tonight.'

Even if a person is just standing on the bridge, looking into the river, they will be approached by a member of the team – just for a chat, to see if they are okay. 'If we even save one person's life, standing out there on those cold nights is all worth it. In the 12 years we've been going, we know of only three cases of the 800 we have saved, who have returned to the river and taken their lives. There have been one or two over the years who we would see come back to the river once or twice a month. We also see some of the people we saved now getting on with their lives.'

'Some of the people are ill. Still you can't be sure – no one comes and announces, "I'm here because of a mental illness." It can be impulsive or planned. Some of the people who we stop throwing themselves over have actually written suicide notes. In order to respect the anonymity of the individuals they have saved, Foyle Search and Rescue don't follow up with them, however, they do make sure they are aware of the organisations available to them, depending on the nature of the person's problem, and will also offer to go along with them.

Foyle Search and Rescue know that their job doesn't end once they have physically stopped someone from throwing themselves into the river. 'When we see someone about to throw themselves over, there's no point in halting them at the railings and saying "safe home".' The Crisis Intervention Team, volunteers who have shown an aptitude in relating to those in crisis and who have good listening skills, seeks firstly to direct a person in danger away from the river to safety. The person is then encouraged to come to the group's headquarters, where they have a counselling room. 'We take them back to the base for a cup of tea and a chat.' Once they are satisfied that the person is no longer at risk, they ensure overnight safety and offer to put them in touch with relevant organisations for counselling and further assistance. 'We let them know that there are organisations out there who can help.' The Crisis Intervention Team is available 24 hours a day, 7 days a week. If the person resists them violently, volunteers call the police, as it is the only way of ensuring that the person will be unable to take their lives that evening.

Paddy says that people are generally quite open and appreciate the chance to talk to someone who will listen. 'Some people want help and ask us to get them into hospital. In such a case, we'll bring them to a doctor for assessment.' Paddy says that a lot of the people they come across have just suffered a crisis in their lives. 'There can be relationship break-ups, even a spur of the moment thing – other times it can be a problem they have been worrying about for a while. Some people tell us they have lost a loved one, sometimes through suicide, and individuals sometimes talk of sexual abuse problems.'

Foyle Search and Rescue say they act like a 4th Emergency Service and the police will often call them when there is a report of a person in the river. The organisation operates a 24-hour call-out service and if someone has gone missing and there are fears that they may be going to end it all, Foyle Search and Rescue will send out the boat. Paddy says there have been cases where people have sent texts to loved ones, saying that they plan to end it all and have gone to the river. In such cases, the Emergency Response Team is dispatched.

The group has a strong belief in the importance of suicide prevention programmes and regularly participates in school visits and talks.

Despite the Trojan work carried out by Foyle Search and Rescue, they can't ultimately stop people from being lost in the river altogether. As a result, the organisation also plays a huge role in helping families to recover their loved ones' bodies. They work together with the individual families, walking along both sides of the river, searching while the tide is low. Sometimes, the search will finish in a matter of hours, but they can often go on for a number of weeks. Foyle Search and Rescue is committed to never calling off the search until they have found the body. They say that the average time required to recover a body is three to four weeks. The body can be in an awful state upon retrieval, which is harrowing for both volunteers and the family, if they choose to see it. The longer the search, the more traumatic for the family concerned. It is bad enough that their loved one has taken their own life, but not having a body prolongs the trauma. The charity does their utmost to alleviate the suffering in so far as they can by providing support and up-to-date information on how the search is progressing.

There are a number of other voluntary organisations throughout Ireland that engage in similar work. David Linehan was just a teenager when he became involved in search and rescue operations on the River Lee in Cork city. Little did he think then that it would fall to him, some years later, to pull his own father's body from the river.

David says you never think something like this will happen in your own family. He recalls listening to a man on the radio making an appeal for information on his missing brother, 'I was getting my hair cut and I heard a local man, Cormac Cremin, talk about his missing brother, Pearse, on the radio. Pearse was a well-known tennis coach in Cork city. I sympathised with him, but I could never have imagined that our family would be in a similar situation in a matter of months.'

David's father, Thomas, worked with Cork Harbour Commission as berthing master. He was used to working on the water and, because of the nature of his work, had sometimes recovered bodies from the harbour. On 3 January 2001, 61-year-old Thomas went missing. His wife, Philomena, raised the alarm and a number of searches got underway. David knew how to search and immediately brought out all the sub aqua groups, the Gardaí and many friends and colleagues, but nothing was found.

Cormac Cremin, whose interview David had listened to on the radio, became one of David's strongest supporters, taking over the task of putting up search posters for Thomas on one side of the city, as well as assisting in the search.

More than three months later, on 14 April, a local man was out picking periwinkles when he discovered a man's foot at the edge of the water. This type of discovery is pretty horrific, but at the same time the family of a missing person welcomes it as it may lead to the location of their loved one's body, which is what happened in this case.

The search for Thomas was then concentrated on the area where the foot had been discovered, with David and the rest of the sub aqua team going through the area meticulously, looking for any clues in the water. Four days later, David found the rest of his father's remains and was able to retrieve them and bring them ashore.

David believes it was a good thing that it was he who found his father as he had done this type of work before and also because he felt privileged in being able to render this last service to his father.

'It had to be done', he said, 'and I was used to that kind of work. It was closure for the family. Finding my father was a relief and we were able to give him a Christian burial.'

Although David says the loss of his father 'destroyed the whole family', he says, 'the worst part of it was when he was missing, the greatest pain of all was not knowing what had happened or where he was. We were heartbroken when his remains were found but we were glad to find out something. So many people go for years without knowing what has happened to a loved one.'

When his own father disappeared, David felt keenly the lack of resources available to assist in the search for missing persons and the delay in getting a search underway. But 'rather than whinge about it', as he puts it himself, 'I felt it was up to us to do something to make things better, to have better communications with those involved.' David immediately set about making contact with the various rescue services, the dog unit and the divers, bringing them all together.

Today, the rescue services in the Cork area are well co-ordinated, ready to go into search mode at a moment's notice and will travel all over the country if necessary. Sadly, they have recovered six bodies from the River Lee and two years ago, they assisted local services in searching the River Slaney in Enniscorthy, Co. Wexford, where five people were missing in separate incidents, recovering two of them.

The first thing volunteers with Foyle Search and Rescue will do upon recovering a body from the river is say a prayer over it and then get permission from the police to move the body to shore. Foyle Search and Rescue has to ensure that the search team is physically strong enough to lift the bodies aboard the boat. They bring the body to their lower base where the police will be waiting and a priest is contacted to administer the last rites. 'We stay with the body until the priest and undertaker come along and the person is pronounced dead by the police or by a doctor.' When a body is located, volunteers assist the police and may be called to give evidence at an inquest.

Over the 12 years that the group has been in existence, they have physically prevented 800 people from throwing themselves into the river, rescued 64 from the water and recovered 42 bodies.

Suicide and Prison: Interview with John Lonergan, Governor of Mountjoy Prison

Prisoners are at a higher risk of suicide than the general population. UK research estimates the magnitude of increased risk among prisoners as five times that of the general population.

Still, Governor of Mountjoy prison John Lonergan stresses that the rate of suicide in prisons is not extraordinarily high. At the time of going to print, the latest figures available for prison deaths were for 2003, during which there were a total of nine deaths in custody, of which two appeared to have been self-inflicted. The 2003 Annual Report of the Irish Prison Services states that, in a number of other instances, attempted suicides were prevented by the vigilance of prison staff.

John Lonergan says that suicide may occur as infrequently as once every five years in Mountjoy prison. However, he does stress that '[one] suicide in a prison, even over a five-year period, is one suicide too many. It is becoming a rarer and rarer occurrence, but it still happens.' John Lonergan says that when he started his career in the 1980s, he inherited a very difficult situation and a system with many problems. Prior to the 1980s, very few suicides took place in Irish prisons at all; the 1980s was the first time that prisons were confronted with the many issues surrounding suicide, including the stigmatisation, the public reaction, the political reaction and the media reaction to suicide in prison. Speaking at a conference on suicide in Ireland, John explained, 'At that stage, there was very little emphasis, if any, on suicide in the community. It is amazing the way the whole thing has moved on since. I suppose I have been there through all those changes.'

John says that in the mid-1980s, there were six deaths in prison over a six-month period, some of which were suicides. 'There was a very bad spell. I can't say for sure that they were suicides because they took substances which poisoned them.'

According to John Lonergan, there are many reasons why the risk of suicide among prisoners is so high. Prison populations can be defined as vulnerable because of a number of different factors. 'Of course, those who end up in prison have to be classified as a vulnerable group for all sorts of reasons. The first thing is the fact that they are confined, the vast number of them against their will. I never say that everybody is confined against their will because we do come across some very sad situations, where people actually almost volunteer to go to prison because of their circumstances outside. I suppose that is sadder still, but for the vast [majority] of people, they are there against their will and that automatically makes them different.'

The fact that people in prison have committed crimes attaches a huge stigma to the individual, as well as to the family and community they have come from. Owing to the nature of the underworld that prisoners are often connected to, they may be threatened, for example, if they haven't paid up money as expected. In such instances, Lonergan says they are reluctant to talk about it or go into protection. Communication and the ability to talk about problems is considered a protective factor against suicide – in many instances, where their safety is being threatened, prisoners are not in a position to discuss their problems and seek help, without putting themselves at further risk in their own minds. Another risk factor is the hopelessness felt by many prisoners with long sentences and very little to look forward to, other than years behind bars. 'It's the whole environment in prison. Prisoners can spend 16–17 hours a day locked in a cell on their own. Lock-up times are the high-risk periods. It was even worse before television. Television has some benefit as it occupies people.'

Dr John Connolly of the Irish Association of Suicidology points out that too much time to brood can be a problem and a contributory factor in suicide. Lonergan says there are lots of people in prison that have served 25 and 26 years of a life sentence and they are no nearer to getting out. 'We are brilliant at commenting about things like they should serve long sentences, 20 or 30 years. But 25 years is a hell of a long time. Look forward 25 years and say what is going to happen. Most people would be gone in 25 years. Look at the changes that will happen in one year. Can you imagine looking forward to 25 years or 20 years or whatever it is? That has nothing got to do with whether the person deserves it or not. I am just talking about some of the immediate things that people are confronted with.'

There is also a high level of depression and mental illness among the prisoner community. 'One in four of all prisoners in Mountjoy prison have a history of being an in-patient in psychiatric hospitals.' Feelings of fear can be particularly high when a prisoner is due to leave prison as they don't know what to expect on the outside. They carry the stigma of having been in prison and they are aware that they may be confronted with a negative reaction in their communities and in the world of work – that is if they can get a job. These types of fears and the sense of isolation they can create can contribute to the sense of hopelessness connected to suicide.

John Lonergan also points out that about 600 of the 3,300 people in prison on any one day have not been sentenced. 'They are people in custody, awaiting sentence and they are probably the highest risk of all of the 3,300 because of the fact that they are on remand.' A huge number of prisoners also suffer from alcohol or drug addiction, which are further risk factors for suicide.

Lonergan says the death of a prisoner is always a big issue. 'If they take their own life, it's a bigger issue.' He refers to the expectation that if someone is removed from society and put in prison, they are automatically safe from harm, including self-inflicted harm. Thus, even though suicides have become so rampant in the wider community, prison suicides still hit the headlines.

A lot has been done to prevent suicide in prisons; however, Lonergan says that despite their best efforts, if someone is determined to take their own lives, you can't stop them unless you monitor them 24 hours a day. 'We have learned from harsh experience that multiple people in a cell is no protection, either.' There has been a case of a person hanging themselves, while the others in the cell slept. 'The new prisons don't have bars. One of the reasons they were eliminated is suicide. They can't use them to hang from, whereas previously they could tie a rope to them.'

A number of initiatives have been put in place to target the problem of suicide in prison. 'Every quarter, there is an awareness meeting on suicide prevention. All disciplines meet (teachers, guards, nurses, governors, psychiatrists) to discuss all incidences: attempted suicide and incidences of people being moved to padded cells. It's monitored every quarter and the forum meets in the immediate aftermath of a suicide as well. Lots of different strategies are put in place, such as padded cells. [There is a lot of] accumulation of information.'

Lonergan says there is also a lot more awareness around staff training and signs of someone being at high risk. 'We would be on the look out if a prisoner was awake during the night or if people were retiring to their cells during the day. There was a case a few years ago of a young officer checking on a prisoner at night-time, who aroused suspicions in his mind, and he came back a little while later and saw him hanging and was able to save him.' Still, at night-time it is impossible to watch every single prisoner at every moment. 'During the stillness of the night from 8 pm on, the night guards are trying to monitor 500 men and it's impossible to give them all full-time attention and observation.'

The prisoner population is made up overwhelmingly of young males between their late teens and mid-thirties. In terms of overall suicide rates for Ireland, these age and gender groups have the highest rates.

In recent years, considerable efforts have been made to bring about a reduction in both self-harm and suicide in prisons. Steps taken include the introduction of methadone maintenance in 2002. To reduce isolation and loneliness in cells, televisions have been introduced. Meanwhile, psychiatric services in prisons have also been significantly improved. While previously there was a much longer wait for psychiatric help, there are now three to four sessions per week, each three hours long. The provision of two full-time psychologists in the male prison and one in the female prison ensures increased assistance to prisoners who want to talk about their problems and receive professional help. Also of crucial importance, according to Lonergan, is the chaplaincy service, which consists of four full-time Catholic clergymen and one full-time Church of Ireland clergyman. Lonergan says that chaplains are particularly important to dislocated people who are guilty of sexual offences. For these prisoners who, owing to the nature of their offence, have little support on the outside and can often be shunned by fellow prisoners, the contact that the chaplaincy service offers is absolutely essential. Ongoing staff training has also resulted in greater awareness around suicide.

The way the media handles suicide in prisons can be very insensitive and John feels there is often a total lack of respect for the dead person and their family. 'Their criminal record and their whole history is broadcast.' When a prisoner dies by suicide, the public's reaction can be callous: they can perceive the death of a 'trouble-maker' as no great loss, which adds greatly to the grieving family's trauma. 'There is no recognition that that person has children, a father, a mother. A prisoner's family suffers emotionally and psychologically, as well. It's just as traumatic for them and there's no respect for that.'

John does believe it is very important that suicide in prison receives attention because, in modern society, the issue of suicide is often brushed under the carpet. He feels that the reporting of suicide in prisons raises awareness of the whole issue, though he would prefer the reporting was more sensitive across the board. 'A prisoner's suicide is a failure on behalf of the prison service – it's important to recognise that we failed to protect that person's life. It's very hard to make it foolproof.' John points out that suicide in prison is still extremely rare;

the fact that it receives so much publicity may give the impression that it is more common. There were no suicides in Mountjoy in 2004, the year prior to my interview with John. He also emphasises that a number of suicides have been prevented in Mountjoy and other Irish prisons, but these stories don't make the headlines. 'A lot of people have been saved here.'

John believes that society can be very harsh on the prison community, many of whom are very vulnerable individuals, and he is adamant that none of us has the right to point the finger at anybody else. 'I don't care who we are. None of us have the right to. There is not one of us an inch away from being vulnerable ourselves. Not one of us. We just pay lip-service to people who are in difficulty [and to] some of the social issues [and] some of the human issues, like suicide. As a society, we pay lip-service to it like we paid lip-service to the drug addiction problems in Dublin for years; like we pay lip-service to the unfortunate people lying on trolleys now in hospitals.' John believes it is essential to take action on the issue of suicide, saying conferences are a waste of time and space if we don't do something.

Philip McTaggart

Philip McTaggart from North Belfast was just 17 when he died by suicide on 23 April 2003. Philip was due to turn 18 on 7 September 2003. His dad, also Philip, was due to celebrate his 40th in July of the same year and his dad recalls sadly how the two had planned to celebrate their important birthdays together by going for a pint as soon as Philip had reached the legal age.

Philip's death came as a complete shock to his father and he still doesn't know what caused him to do something so drastic. Philip and his father got on very well. Philip had lived with his mother since his parents split up when he was three, but he stayed with his dad on occasion at weekends and went on holidays with him. As Philip got older, he came over to visit his dad more regularly. Both parents had remarried. As groomsman at his father's wedding, Philip made a hilarious speech. 'He was a very witty young lad.'

Despite the normal challenges of life, things had appeared to be going well for Philip. His dad says he was a good-looking lad. 'He dressed very well – all the girls fancied him! He was a very, very confident person. I would almost have loved to have been like that myself.'

Philip left school at 16 years of age and started to work in a bar. His father was not happy with his decision to leave school. 'I was pretty annoyed. I told him that when his friends were out enjoying themselves or off on holiday, he would be working. We would have fallen out on issues like that. We didn't see eye to eye on the subject.'

After a while, Philip left the bar and went to work with his father in the building trade. 'At the beginning of the summer, I said, "enjoy July and August because you're coming to work with me in September".' His dad organised for Philip to become part of a training scheme and he was earning decent money. 'He got on alright but didn't particularly like it. It was good for him, though, to see how hard work was. He stuck it out for about eight months and then we had a chat. I could see he didn't like it. He never missed a day but he had no interest. I said to him, "What would you like to do?"'

Philip decided he wanted to get into hairdressing and become a barber. He loved it. 'He said, "There's a girls' school across the street. It's great."' Philip enjoyed the social aspect of hairdressing, talking to different people as he worked. His father said that Philip seemed very happy with his choice of employment. 'He had only been there for a couple of months and had already gone out and bought good equipment – a scissors etc. He wanted to do it and do it right.' His family was delighted to see Philip getting on so well and starting a career. 'I told him once he was qualified he could go out and set up on his own. I was delighted for him. As his father, I wanted to make sure he was okay and had the means to earn a living. He was very intelligent but, like a lot of young people, he didn't want to stay in school or go to college. I wasn't happy that he left school, but thought that maybe in his twenties he might change his mind.'

His dad felt that Philip was one of the lucky ones in that he had a job. 'I know a number of people who can't get a job in the area. There is a pretty poor employment rate in the area; a lot of young people are unemployed.' But Philip had a job, loads of friends and a girlfriend. 'There was no sign whatsoever that there was something seriously wrong.'

Philip died on Easter Tuesday. In the days leading up to his death, he had appeared to be in great form. 'He was up in my house on Easter Sunday and Easter Monday and he was laughing and joking away. Himself and his girlfriend came down to me to see the kids, Tomás and Émer, and brought them Easter eggs. We were laughing as the kids were only one year old. I have twins, a boy and a girl, who are now three.'

Philip left his father's house on Easter Sunday, apparently in high spirits. Philip Senior has pieced together the last hours of his son's life from talking to his friends. He had been up in his mother's house in the afternoon. His mum was out and he had some wine; he drank roughly half a bottle.

At about 6.30 pm he went out for a walk with a couple of friends, not really going anywhere in particular. His friends said he was in great form. They walked to the bottom end of Ardoyne and then something happened. Apparently, Philip and another guy started arguing – his father doesn't know exactly what happened or why the argument started. 'The details are all very sketchy, but something happened there and it ended up in a row. Philip then went off and his friend said he would drive him around to meet up with his girlfriend.' Philip got into the car and chatted away about plans for the following evening. 'They were talking about going weight-training the next night. Philip was talking about the future, and was in good form in the car.'

It was about 8 pm when Philip got out of the car to meet up with his girlfriend, who was out in an area where her friends lived. Philip Senior says there is very little for young people to do in the Ardoyne area, so they would generally meet up and walk around the area. Philip said goodbye to his friend, calling out, 'See you tomorrow night,' as his friend drove away.

His dad says he doesn't have a clear picture of what followed. 'It all gets a bit cloudy here. There seemed to be another argument and Philip's whole attitude and thinking changed. Philip ended up in a really bad way emotionally. He was crying and started saying he was going to kill himself. It was around 10 o'clock or so.' Some people said they thought that Philip was drunk. 'He was crying a lot, and staggering and kicking things on the ground. The way it was explained to me I thought he had to have been on drugs.' Philip's friends were concerned by his behaviour so they called his mother, who arrived and tried to comfort Philip and persuade him to go home with her, but Philip wouldn't. Someone told Philip they were going up to get his dad but Philip said, "I don't want my daddy involved".' Philip Senior feels his son may not have wanted to worry him as he and his wife had recently had the twins. It was at this point that Philip left the group and went off on his own.

Philip's girlfriend went to Philip Senior's house to get help. He was out at the time but his wife rang him and told him that Philip was in a bad way and he was saying he was going to kill himself. Knowing Philip, his dad thought that his behaviour was very unusual and figured his son had probably been in a row and had a few drinks; but he didn't imagine for a moment that Philip was seriously thinking of taking his life. They went out to look for him – Philip Senior on foot and his wife, Kelley, in the car. Kelley rang Philip's mobile. He answered, crying and sobbing. When she asked him where he was, he kept saying, 'I'm up here and I'm going to kill myself'. Kelley told him that his dad was out looking for him and told him that whatever the problem was, they would work it out.

Philip just kept repeating that he was going to do it. Then, he seemed to regain his composure. Kelley asked him again where he was and said they were coming to get him. He just said, 'I'm up here' and he hung up. It was about a quarter to midnight. Philip Senior went to Philip's mother's house and they all went out to look for him. They went to every high point they could think of in the area. 'We tried to go over everything he had said. I was convinced he must have been on drugs or drink because this was completely out of character. This was not the son I knew. We searched everywhere.'

They continued to look for Philip into the early hours and contacted his friends to see if anyone had any idea where he could be. They were extremely worried, but Philip Senior still did not imagine for a moment that his son would have taken his life. From what he learned about Philip's behaviour that evening, his dad was convinced that there had to have been a high level of drink or drugs involved and expected that his son would wake up in a friend's house the next day. They didn't call the police, but Philip Senior explains that you would have to come from their area to understand this. 'Where we live, there is still a lack of trust between the police and the community. It's not something people in the area would automatically do.'

At about 10.30 am the next day, Philip Senior got a phone call from Philip's aunt. She told him to come up to the house quickly – the priest was there. His Dad thought she said the *police*. 'I thought he was in some trouble, but as I was driving up to the house I started to think did she say *priest* or *police*?'

'I started to put the speed on and arrived at his aunt's house in a matter of minutes. As I drove in, I noticed about four women standing on a street corner. This is something you never like to see and my heart started to race. I realised something was really wrong here.' Philip's aunt opened the front door and told Philip Senior to come in. 'I got into the hallway and heard Philip's Mammy screaming crying. I said to Philip's aunt, "Don't be telling me Philip's dead" and she said, "Yes he is, he's dead."'

Philip immediately rang his wife, Kelley, who was just about to head out again to look for Philip. She started screaming and Philip's girlfriend, who was in the house with Kelley, started screaming as well. Philip Senior wanted to go and see the body. He couldn't believe that his son was dead.

His body was in the church grounds. Philip Senior hurried out to the car. Fr Aidan Troy, who had broken the news to Philip's mother, came after him. A friend of the family, he got into the car with Philip Senior and told him he was coming with him.

'I said to Aidan, "I don't think it's Philip."' Fr Aidan told him it was. 'I said, "I have to see if it's Philip. I need to see him."'

Philip had been found in the Church grounds after ten o'clock mass. He was in an area of trees called the Grove at the back of the chapel. The area was known as being dangerous, especially late at night as the ground was an interface between the Catholic and Protestant communities and there was a lot of tension between the two. The Holy Cross dispute had taken place in Ardoyne not long before and, at the time of Philip's death, there was still a lot of trouble with pipe bombs and petrol bombs. 'It was a very scary place to be.'

Two local men had been on their way to pick up some gardening tools for the priest when they came across the body. At first they thought it was someone coming through from the other side and they ducked. Then they realised it was the body of a young man and they immediately ran and got the priest, Fr Brendan, who gave the last rites. 'When I arrived, the PSNI had arrived and had put Philip in a body bag.' He had hanged himself from the tree with a piece of pipe. As there was a cut on Philip's knuckle, they said they had to treat it as an investigation for forensics and they couldn't show his dad the body. Philip Senior insisted that he needed to see the body, and they said he could go to the morgue later that day.

Philip Senior headed home to his house. Word of what had happened had obviously spread in the tight-knit community and the house was full of neighbours and people were making tea and sandwiches. 'I didn't know what was going on. I was just crying. I remember a sensation of pins and needles running down my arm. I was just hoping there had been some mistake. I needed to see him.' They phoned the morgue to check that Philip's body was there and Fr Aidan Troy drove Philip Senior, his wife, Kelley, and a friend over to see him. When they arrived at the morgue, Philip Senior was shown his son's clothes and he realised it was Philip. He was brought in to see the body, but told not to touch him.

'When I saw him it looked as if he was sleeping. Fr Troy said some prayers ... I just stared and stared and walked away and then I said, "Fuck, that is my son". I went back and kissed his forehead ... I remember saying, "Why did you do it?" At that stage, shock really hit ... I couldn't think straight. I was crying. I couldn't get my act together ... and was constantly going over and over in my head what had happened.' Once again, Philip Senior had a sensation of pins and needles running down his arms and legs as he tried to comprehend the fact that his 17-year-old son really had died by suicide. 'It is the most unbelievable feeling, the most horrible thing anyone can go through and I wouldn't wish it on my worst enemy.'

Philip Senior still can't understand why his son would take his life. 'He was a bubbly young person and had been looking forward to driving lessons he was starting and his holidays. He wasn't diagnosed with depression and showed no signs of suffering from depression. He was always in good form.' He had plenty of people to talk to. Philip Senior was convinced that the autopsy would reveal that Philip had taken a lot of drink or drugs. His dad knew that Philip drank sometimes: 'He would have a drink in the corner and a smoke like any other young lad. I never saw him drunk, but then I didn't see him all the time.' The autopsy, however, revealed that the amount of alcohol in Philip's system made him less than two times over the legal driving limit. There were no drugs involved. Philip's death was certified as suicide and no inquest was held. The family was asked whether they wanted an inquest and, feeling they wouldn't learn anything new from it and rather than go through the pain and trauma all over again, they decided against it. In the North, holding an inquest in the case of suicide is at the Coroner's discretion.

There was a huge turn-out at Philip's funeral. Philip Senior was stunned by the number of people who approached him and said that their son or daughter had attempted to take their lives and he realised what a serious problem it was. He learned that, in recent years, the rate of suicide in North Belfast was one of the highest in Europe. He feels that Philip's suicide may be connected to a range of problems facing the youth of North Belfast.

'There is massive deprivation in the area we live in. There are no facilities for young people – there are no green areas for them to go to. Furthermore, there are a huge number of people on housing waiting lists, many of these [are] crisis waiting lists. Houses are being built on every green area. In our area of Ardoyne, we have about seven interface walls that split the Catholic and Protestant communities. There are major problems and there is huge tension in the community especially in the summer, during the marching season.'

More than half the population of the Ardoyne are under the age of 18. The effects of the Troubles and the trauma of the Holy Cross dispute inevitably take a psychological toll, particularly on young people. 'It was a major, major issue and we haven't even tapped into the problems all those young girls and families will have as they get older. The high levels of youth suicide are symptomatic of the problems the community faces.' The suicide rate in the North went up when the peace process came in. During times of conflict, communities bond together and with the end of conflict, society opens up much more and people are exposed to other pressures. Though the rates of suicide fell during the Troubles, there were still more deaths by suicide during those 30 years than there were deaths that were a direct result of the Troubles.

Philip McTaggart Senior has now set up a support group called PIPS (Public Initiative for the Prevention of Suicide and Self-harm), a project dedicated to the memory of his son, who was nicknamed Pip by his friends.

The organisation aims to help young people contemplating suicide or self-harm, to create greater awareness of services available to those considering suicide and to give support to families who have lost a loved one. The organisation is a cross-community initiative and provides support to both Protestant and Catholic families. Philip believes the organisation has already saved a number of lives. Volunteer counsellors are on call 24 hours a day to give advice to families and young people in crisis. He is conscious that they can't prevent every single suicide, but they feel a vast amount can be done.

'We have to make sure there are facilities for young people and proper medical services must be available. We need to keep putting pressure on both governments. The reason this whole subject has been brought to the table is because families who have lost loved ones are putting pressure on both governments.'

The Health Secretary for Northern Ireland has commissioned a report due out in 2006 on the situation regarding suicide in the North. Philip Senior hopes that the report will result in money being allocated to a task force on suicide. 'We want to see this money going into the community. If we work together with health professionals in tackling this issue, we can bring the rate of suicide down dramatically.'

PIPS received funding to organise Applied Suicide Intervention Skills Training (ASIST) training for a number of people in the organisation, with the result that six members became trainers themselves and have since trained over 300 others to become ASIST volunteers. 'Right at this minute, those people are being contacted by letter to ask them if they are still interested in becoming a prevention volunteer. It's a trial programme we are putting in place just in North Belfast. There will be a group of ASIST volunteers in each area and each group will have a mobile phone, so if there's an issue in that community, if a family loses someone or someone is saying they will take their lives, a quick response team will go directly to the person's home to offer advice and support straight away – this could even be financial support to get that person professional help, or the volunteers may direct them to the right person where possible.'

PIPS is also trying to encourage teachers to do the ASIST training and, like many other suicide prevention organisations, they are campaigning to have 'emotional well-being classes' added to the curriculum. 'Instead of it all being about the capability of the young person in terms of exams, we are arguing that students should also be taught how to deal with their feelings. We want young people to be helped and advised in dealing with relationships and to be taught [that] it's alright to feel, it's alright to cry.' Philip Senior is adamant that young people need to be taught coping skills at school level, so they are prepared for the real world of dealing with relationships, job-hunting and the general challenges of life. 'They need to be prepared to deal with the challenges that lie at every corner and understand that life isn't all rosy. They need to be taught that some times will be harder than others. Every school should also have a trained and professional counsellor.'

Philip Senior is also adamant that suicide should be discussed more openly. 'People don't understand it and no one wants to bring it home. Before Philip's death, suicide was a taboo subject for me. I didn't understand it. It's the silent killer. It doesn't matter if you're Protestant, Catholic, rich or poor, it affects everyone. At least if we have some skills to detect if there's something wrong, we can do something about it.'

Philip Senior believes listening and allowing young people to talk is the key to preventing suicide. 'To adults, a person's problems at 17 may seem trivial to us and we can brush them off. Nowadays, everyone is so busy. In most families, both parents are mostly working and in their spare time, they have so much else on the agenda, whether it's doing the shopping or going for a game of golf. Your child could say something to you [when you are] on the way out the door. You need to stop and turn around and sit down with them. Forget the shopping, forget the golf and say to them, "explain it to me." Even though they may laugh about it in a year or two's time, at that moment, it's a big thing.'

Philip Senior says that life has become so fast-paced that there is not enough time in the day anymore. 'We don't hug our children as much as we used to. We need to turn around and start talking more and listening is the big thing. If I had turned around to Philip at the time and asked him what was wrong, maybe we could have sorted it out ... but he never said anything that set the alarm bells racing.' Philip Senior also believes we need to be more encouraging, especially of young males.

'Sometimes we need to step back and look at things a wee bit differently and relax a wee bit and show them a bit of respect and trust.'

PIPS also provides bereavement support groups to families touched by suicide. Family and neighbours were very good to the McTaggart family when Philip died. Philip Senior says Fr Aidan Troy and Fr Gary Donovan have been a major support to him, in terms of sitting down and talking and going through all of the issues with him. 'Fr Aidan was a family friend. He knew Philip and he hurried home from Larne to Belfast once he heard and stuck by me that whole day.'

Philip Senior still asks himself every single day why his son did it. He misses him terribly and is distraught not to be able to see him grow into adulthood. Not a day passes that he doesn't cry for Philip. He says nothing as bad could ever happen to him again. 'No matter what life throws at me or at Philip's mother, nothing can ever be as bad as what happened. I used to have a fear of dying, but nothing could be as frightening as going through my son's suicide. Of course I don't want to die; I have a family and value my life. I'm just saying that the pain, anguish, hurt and trauma of Philip's death could never be experienced as a result of anything else.'

Suicide and Schizophrenia

Suicide is the biggest premature killer among people who suffer from schizophrenia. An overwhelming 10 per cent of all people who are diagnosed with schizophrenia die by suicide. People who suffer from schizophrenia can face serious problems and their whole attitude to life can change to the point where they no longer feel there is any point in living. Research has shown that people with schizophrenia are more vulnerable to suicide than any other group in the population (Schizophrenia Ireland).

It is vital to stress here that a diagnosis of schizophrenia does not necessarily mean that a lifelong illness is inevitable. People do improve and recover and hope is regarded as an essential ingredient in this recovery. The Schizophrenia Ireland (SI) website (www.sirl.ie) provides links to a number of recovery stories, which can be very helpful to individuals in crisis who fear things will never improve.

The story of Tim, who was diagnosed with schizophrenia 20 years ago, when he was 24, is a case in point. It took him a couple of years to accept that he had an illness and he has been in hospital six times since. Apart from the 'high' symptoms, Tim says he also had delusions. 'I believed people in radio and television were referring to me. I believed I was being filmed by satellite. While I was ill, I would not disclose these delusions to anyone.'

Tim's illness resulted in the break-up of three long-term relationships. Overall, however, Tim considers himself lucky as his symptoms are relatively mild. 'Medication works for me, without side effects, and on the whole, I have been able to work full-time. In the past, I taught English as a foreign language [and] worked as a programmer and technical author. I am presently working in the mental health field.'

'Whenever I did have to go back to hospital, it was either due to stress bringing on the symptoms again or not taking my medication. At the moment, my work is mostly stress-free and I enjoy it. I am receiving a monthly injection, which means that I do not have to remember to take medication daily.'

'In the past, I was earning a lot, spending a lot and generally not facing my problems. I am glad I have found a niche in mental health and I also attribute this to no longer experiencing depressions.'

'Although schizophrenia is only a minor part of my life, it has affected my life hugely. Relationships and work would have been easier [if I didn't suffer from schizophrenia] and I would probably have settled into a career structure by now. On the positive side, however, it has made me more sensitive to other people. I feel I have integrated my illness into my life. Even if I do become ill again, I will be able to bounce back more quickly than before.' (Tim's story is taken from www.recover.ie and is reproduced here with his permission and that of SI.)

Tim's story shows that despite the serious effects of schizophrenia over a person's lifetime, there are good reasons to be optimistic about the future. Early recognition and treatment of schizophrenia can have a significant impact on the medium- and long-term outcomes for someone experiencing their first psychotic episode and also helps their family. Early intervention can result in less frequent admission to hospital, shorter periods of in-patient care, more rapid and complete recovery, a decreased risk of relapse over the following two years and fewer problems in treating the psychosis.

Why are people who suffer from schizophrenia such a high-risk group? Up to 90 per cent of people who take their own lives are suffering from a psychiatric illness. Dr Tony Bates points out that we know that people reach the point of taking their own lives when they feel desperately trapped by their particular circumstances and can see no possibility of escaping their predicament and no likelihood of rescue. He poses the question, 'Could it be that schizophrenia leaves a person more vulnerable to feeling this way?'

Schizophrenia will generally begin with an episode of psychosis. Director of SI, John Saunders, explains psychosis as the onset of an episode of destructive, disorganised behaviour. 'An episode of psychosis can last a couple of weeks or months.' Schizophrenia is when this behaviour is prolonged over a period of time, i.e. for six months or longer. John points out that many people can have psychosis, but get over it and return to a normal life. 'It used to be called a nervous breakdown. Thousands and thousands of people have no incident ever again and go on to a full recovery.'

Psychosis can make people more vulnerable to suicidal behaviour. 'Their thinking becomes disorganised: logical goes to illogical, reality to unreality. They see, hear, smell and have tactile feelings that are not actually there.' He explains that their thinking becomes deluded and they have false beliefs. Paranoia and feelings of fear are very typical. 'They can feel, for example, that someone is following them who will hurt them. They can have strange feelings that they have huge influence on certain situations.'

John has met me in a Dublin hotel for our interview and to clarify this sense of influence, he tells me it would be like believing that, walking into the hotel to meet him, I could cause terrible harm. 'You have delusions about the effect you have on the world.' SI defines delusions as false personal beliefs held with extraordinary conviction, in spite of what others believe and in spite of obvious proof or evidence to the contrary. 'For example, a person experiencing delusions may believe that thoughts are being inserted into their mind or that they have special powers or are someone famous (for example, Jesus Christ or Elvis). People may also think that they are being spied on, tormented, followed or tricked, or may believe that gestures or comments are directed specifically at them. Delusions will occur during some stage of the disorder in 90 per cent of people who experience schizophrenia.'

Obviously, the effects of the illness will have tremendous consequences on the life of an individual and John explains that it can frequently result in the breakdown of personal relationships, the break-up of marriages, as well as in the disintegration of careers. All of the personal life difficulties mentioned here are considered risk factors for suicide, and as people suffering from schizophrenia are more likely to be faced with these personal problems, the risk potential for suicide is much higher. John says that the person is faced with a chaotic future and can feel that there is no way out.

He describes it as particularly hard when a person is newly diagnosed with the illness. As with most mental illness and the attached stigma, people do not want to believe that they have the illness. 'The post-diagnosis scenario is a difficult realisation. Initially people don't accept it and, then, as they do, they realise what the future will be like and they can feel like they don't want to go on.'

He also points out that there is a very strong association between psychosis and depression. 'The presence of depression is often a factor that will drive someone to suicide. At its deepest level, clinical depression strips away the survival instinct and people who reach that point are not worried about living or dying, they don't care if they don't eat and they might actually do something about putting an end to their lives.'

John also points out that many people who die by suicide have been found to be strong users of alcohol, and says that alcohol is frequently used in severe illness, as are illicit drugs. 'It's a way of escaping, of getting a high, but it causes other problems.'

WHO DEVELOPS SCHIZOPHRENIA?

According to SI, people usually develop schizophrenia between the ages of 15 and 34 years. Men have a tendency to develop the condition about five to ten years earlier than women. Schizophrenia can also begin later in life and, although rare, can occur in children. The onset of a psychotic episode may be gradual or rapid, but the majority of individuals display some early signs and symptoms – often referred to as the 'something is not quite right' phase. During this time, people may withdraw from their family and friends, have changes in their appetite and sleep patterns, find it difficult to concentrate and as a result, have difficulties at school, work or in the home. The person may find this period very disturbing, even frightening, and may not want to talk about what is happening to them. This period is referred to in medical language as the 'prodrome' and its length can be anything from a month to several years.

John says that typically women seem to cope better than men. 'They talk more and rely on personal relationships with each other or with males. They are more resilient to ups and downs, while men don't talk. Men have a macho image; they hide things and use drink and drugs to escape.' While schizophrenia occurs among men and women, John says that men cope less well with severe illness.

It is a known fact that those who die by suicide include a significant portion of people who suffer from severe mental illness. Some of these inviduals had been diagnosed with or were suffering from mental illness prior to their deaths.

According to John, the mental health service in Ireland operates on the basis of two assumptions: the first being that they can diagnose severe illness and the second that they can treat and maintain it. 'They haven't factored suicide prevention into that.' He feels that individuals are not monitored enough at the high-risk post-discharge times. 'There is evidence to suggest that [some] people who took their lives, had in the 14 days before they died, talked to mental health professionals. Health care professionals are not currently tuned in to people. Post-discharge is a terrible time for people when they realise what's happened. They're not monitored enough – probably because of resource issues.'

John feels that while there is a lot that we don't know about suicide, we do know that people with mental illness and with schizophrenia, in particular, are more at risk of suicide than the general population and he believes that more should be done to reduce the risk and treat these groups which have been identified.

In 2004 SI launched their 'Life Hope' programme, with the aim of increasing awareness about suicide, about its relationship with severe mental illness and about its prevention; they also offer enhanced counselling for both relatives and persons with self-experience.

John explains 'Life Hope' as a very practical project with a focus on changing attitudes and sharing personal stories. 'For many it is extremely powerful to hear of someone's personal struggles with schizophrenia and feelings of suicidal ideation. Fundamentally, each of these stories have been one of hope – hope that life can and will improve.'

John feels that there has been a perception within the Irish health service that severe mental illness is, somehow, 'for life'. However, he says that this is now changing and he is hopeful that the future for people who suffer from schizophrenia will be positive. He recommends far more acute interventions earlier. He further stresses that when people are treated, they need very good post-discharge service to make sure that they stay well. 'In Ireland, people are brought into hospital and stabilised by treatment, then let out and left – some do okay. We need to replace a fire brigade approach with a pro-active approach.'

He highlights the role of society at large in realising the seriousness of suicide, which in the past has been an unknown, unpublicised issue. The suicide rate is higher than the rate of deaths in road traffic accidents but it does not receive the same publicity.

REDUCING THE RISK OF SUICIDE AMONG PEOPLE WITH SCHIZOPHRENIA

SI believes the notion of recovery must be the foundation of the mental health services in order to encourage hope. SI stresses the importance of the prominent role of the individual in his or her own recovery. 'The core philosophy associated with recovery is that recovery is not only possible but it is expected [....] What is important is the recognition that everyone has the potential to recover...'

Suicide and the Gay, Lesbian and Bisexual Community

Homosexuality was decriminalised in 1993, which was, interestingly, the same year that suicide was decriminalised. Owing to the social and psychological pressures individuals can be put under because of their homosexuality, suicide is certainly an issue in the gay community. In order to dispel bias and misconceptions, at this point it is essential to stress that the risk factor for suicide in the gay, lesbian and bisexual (GLB) community has nothing to do with sexual orientation itself; rather, it is societal prejudices, which can lead to problems like family arguments, isolation and the fear of physical attack, that may put this community at risk.

When I contacted representatives from the GLB community about the issue of suicide, they felt strongly about it and spokespeople from different organisations from all over Ireland travelled up to Dublin to talk to me about the challenges they face.

Paul Madden of the Southern Gay Men's Health Project reasserted that the fact that someone is gay, lesbian or bisexual does not sign that person up for a life of self-harm; however, the pressures that society places on the GLB community can lead to situations in an individual's life that put them at greater risk of suicide. 'Irish society is extremely Catholic. Schools provide no support for gay or lesbian students and the struggle can lead to depression.'

The 2004 Youth Suicide Prevention: Evidence Briefing (UK and Ireland Public Health Evidence Group) identified young men and women of same-sex orientation as one of a number of high-risk groups for youth suicide. There are no significant statistics available to date, however, on the full extent of the level of vulnerability to suicide of the GLB community. Available data does not take into account the unknown number of people who, unwilling to bear the stigma attached to homosexuality, may take their lives before ever coming out.

A panel discussion on the topic of lesbian, gay, bisexual and transgender (LGBT) youth suicide at Outhouse – Dublin's community and resource centre for lesbian, gay, bisexual and transgender people – found that while it is impossible to even speculate on the percentage of suicides linked to sexual orientation, it would be ridiculous not to factor issues of sexuality into discussion about suicide and preventative measures.

As a marginalised group, often subject to prejudice and both verbal and physical abuse, members of the GLB community are faced with tremendous social challenges, many of which can make individuals vulnerable to suicide.

Bruno Nicolai, a Health Promotion Officer at a Sexual Health Centre, told me of the huge difficulty he had in accepting his sexuality owing to the historic stigma attached to homosexuality in Ireland. 'I didn't want to be gay. I thought no-one would like me. As a result, I became social phobic and then agoraphobic for several years as a teenager.' Paul Madden says that the GLB community in Ireland can be put under a lot of stress as there is huge societal pressure on people not to be homosexual. 'The parents of a gay friend of mine told him they would rather he were dead than gay. Imagine what that does to you when the people who brought you into this world and raised you say that to you!'

Since family instability, interpersonal conflict or loss, breakdown in personal relationships, arguments with family or friends, low self-esteem and bullying are all recognised as potentially increasing vulnerability to self-harm, the stories from the representatives I met with highlight the reasons why the GLB community may be more at risk of suicide than the general population. At the Outhouse panel discussion, Fergal Carroll, a counselling psychologist, said that while it was obvious that LGBT adolescents will face the same stressors as any adolescent, 'in the case of LGBT youth, these stressors are enhanced by the lack of positive role models and positive messages about their sexuality. There are also issues around the education system and the lack of gay-positive messages, and anti-homophobic policies in the school system. This means that as well as internalised negative images, there are external factors that may come into play such as bullying or harassment. All of this at a time of life when pressure to conform is at its highest can increase suicide risk for LGBT youth.'

Paul Madden told me of the huge stress he experienced when trying to hide the fact that he was homosexual from his local community in Monaghan. 'There is huge stress in living in two different worlds. I used to be gay in Dublin and straight in my home town of Monaghan. In Monaghan, there was no place for me. The whole normality of an upbringing is lost – we need schools to normalise it.'

Petra Jäppinen, a development worker with Outhouse, points out that in the current climate there are still only so many GLB individuals that can be reached as a community. 'We can do a lot here in Outhouse, but there are a lot of counties with no support services at all. Before I started working here, I was quite isolated, even though I was only half an hour away from Dublin by train.'

The ability to talk about problems and share them with others is considered a hugely protective factor against suicide. The very fact that, until as recently as 1993, homosexuality was a criminal offence, not only made GLB individuals criminals, but also made homosexuality a taboo subject; consequently, it was very difficult for individuals to talk about sexuality and the emotional turmoil caused by the fact that their sexuality made them a criminal. Paul says that the pressure he was under resulted in him developing psychosomatic tonsillitis, which went once he told his mother the truth. At the time of speaking to Paul, homosexuality had been decriminalised less than 13 years before and the stigma in Ireland was still huge.

Paul says that due to the nature of the job he is in (Southern Gay Men's Health Project), he can be open about his sexuality, and he feels other GLB individuals who can be open in clubs are doing okay, but he says there are many married men who are gay and people who are afraid to ring a helpline. Bruno says his sympathies are with gay people growing up in country towns, miles away from services. Although he says that nowadays, at least these groups have the internet, which makes it a lot easier for them to realise that they're not the only GLB people. According to Paul, the level of difficulty depends on where a person lives. 'Dublin and Cork both have a gay scene.'

Paul feels that as a result of the stigma and the pressure around homosexuality in Ireland, GLB people are struggling with their sexuality and trying to fit into a heterosexual society.

When I attended the STOP conference in Leitrim in February 2005, a youth worker told the conference that he was concerned about the risk of suicide in young gay men, based on the typical reaction to a question he put to school students in various schools through youth work. He reported that when he asked students what they would do if one of their classmates was gay, the general response was that they would 'kick the s**t out of them'. With Paul Madden of the Southern Men's Health Project estimating that 1–3 of every 10 people are gay, such a response would marginalise and seriously challenge the levels of self-esteem of an enormous number of individuals.

Paul believes that the way to challenge the stigma and negative attitude is through education in schools. He feels that fear of stigmatisation, even on the part of teachers, results in students being allowed to poke fun and prejudice at the notion of being homosexual.' "Gay" is a bad word. If someone makes a racist slur in a classroom, it's unacceptable. However, if someone says "gay", "queer" or "fairy", teachers will usually not interfere as they fear being judged "gay by association".' Bernadine Quinn, representing Dundalk Outcomers (a GLB resource centre with various groups), feels that instead of a teacher hiding from the joke of queer, they should ask the student what they mean.

The pressure against being homosexual is constant for a lot of GLB individuals and the psychological effects are significant. According to a 2004 strategy document to promote the mental health of lesbians and gay men, both national and international research indicates that the high level of marginalisation, exclusion and discrimination experienced by lesbians and gay men can have negative effects for both physical and mental health.' However, the report also points out that although research findings show an increased risk of suicide among lesbians and gay men, 'this varies considerably according to individual, social, economic and socio-political circumstances'.

Bruno says that a lot of his gay friends are on medication because of psychological problems resulting from marginalisation and discrimination and fear. 'Anxiety, depression, obsessive compulsive disorder: these were problems which started years ago, when they were not able to come out.' He describes the main problems of GLB people including fear and self-hatred, which he refers to as 'internalised homophobia'. 'No young, gay man in Ireland doesn't have that. They don't know what people's reactions are going to be. This is ingrained from school, and the implications are life-long. You hate yourself for lying.'

Added to the worry of how society will view them, GLB people can be genuinely fearful for their physical safety – Paul says that a lot of hate crimes against GLB people go unreported and Bruno says that this fear can affect even tiny aspects of a person's life. 'You have to worry about what you wear and ask yourself, *Am I looking a bit camp today?* It's like being back at school – you're okay in a gay club but not walking down O'Connell Street in Dublin.' The Gardaí have taken positive moves to reduce this problem and they now have GLB liaison officers, training students in Templemore.

Ciaran McKinney from Gay HIV Strategies says that while working in the area of HIV/AIDS in the UK, he knew a number of gay people who died by reckless death or by suicide. He stresses, however, that there are millions and millions of GLB people throughout the world who have no such problems and says that it is important to recognise this because, in the past, psychiatry and psychology classified GLB people as mentally unwell. This is no longer the case. In western psychiatry, homosexuality per se has been demedicalised, just as it has been decriminalised. Ciaran points out that any sub-community, including the Irish community in the UK, has a much higher rate of self-harm and suicide, a fact that has, in the past, been used by some to say that Irish people are mentally unstable.

This generalisation ignores the stress factors associated with loneliness, isolation, poor integration within society, and so on. GLB people may, as a result of having been made to feel abnormal in society, experience suicidal thoughts or engage in deliberate self-harm. Many of the representatives who gathered to talk to me felt it very important not to label the GLB community as a whole as being at risk from suicide. While many present agreed that suicide was an issue as a result of the societal pressures on GLB people in Ireland, they stressed that there were many factors that affected both suicide and mental health. 'In the 1960s, 1970s and 1980s, it wouldn't have been uncommon for people to be on tranquillisers because of deprivation or for other reasons.'

Meanwhile, Bernadine said that a large number of people who have used Dundalk Outcomers over the years have been a visitor to a psychiatrist and have been treated for depression. 'In the past eight years, there have sadly been some deaths as a result of suicide among those attending our organisation.'

Bernadine says the centre is attended by a number of people who have made attempts on their lives. From the experiences these people have shared at the centre, it appears that their attempted suicides were related to their sexuality and to the fears imposed by society. 'I think it has to be the fear of coming out; this side of it, you realise there's a better life after coming out. It's frustrating trying to get that point across.'

Billie from the Red Ribbon Project (a voluntary non-profit organisation which provides prevention, care and support services related to HIV/Aids and Sexual Health in the Mid-West of Ireland) says that she tried to take her life following rejection by her parents due to her sexuality. 'I was in a small village after being rejected by my parents and thrown out. It was horrible. I had no money, no love and no parents.' Billie stresses that her attempt on her life was not about her sexuality, rather it was about a lack of hope. Billie feels that other GLB people may ask themselves, when they look outside and see the challenges that will face them, 'Do I want to walk that road?' They may feel that their only choice is either not to be gay or to end it all.

Bruno spoke of an indirect homophobia as everything is geared towards heterosexual people, even sex education in schools. Another indirect form of homophobia can be a simple question from a relative about being given a 'day out', as this applies to a heterosexual wedding and, like many similar comments or situations, can cause discomfort to a GLB person. Bruno says, 'We learn about what heterosexual people do. We live in a heterosexual world.' This raises the further issue of doctors not being tuned in to the fact that psychological problems can be caused by prejudices against a GLB individual. Paul says that doctors wouldn't know how to identify the problems. 'People don't go to doctors and say, "I'm gay". They go because they may feel depressed.'

The group said that the lack of training that counsellors receive around sexuality issues means that professionals dealing with psychological problems or suicide risk are not tuned in to the pressures on the GLB community. Billie points out that asking a person if he or she is gay is almost as hard as asking if they are suicidal. 'All that person might need is to be asked that question.' Bernadine says that GLB people can be afraid of coming out to doctors, especially to a family doctor. 'When that is the root cause of your problems, it can be put down to different issues as you are afraid to say it.'

Bernadine says it is vital that the Health Service is not afraid to say the words 'gay' and 'lesbian'. 'People have got to mention the word "lesbian" or "gay" because if we don't, heterosexuals certainly won't. Teachers are afraid to. They need to be picked and trained so they are not afraid to go in and say what has to be said.' Bernadine sees such training as essential if the stigma is to be reduced in schools, highlighting that currently the biggest insult that can be graffitied on a school wall is 'Mary is a lezzer. Everything else is okay.' She says that teachers need back-up too and referred to the example of a lesbian teacher in an Irish school, who had her car destroyed, and her door kicked in and people shouting 'lezzer' at her, when it was discovered that she was homosexual.

Through the Sexual Health Centre, some work is carried out in schools, Bruno explains. 'Teachers will tell us what they want covered and we tell the teachers we'll answer anything we're asked.' In order to give students the opportunity to ask questions they may not wish to ask in front of their peers, they are invited to write confidential questions on post-it notes. Michael Barron is a Youth Worker with BeLonG To, a youth project, funded by the Department of Education, which was set up in March 2003 for LGBT young people. He says that it is essential to distribute information in schools: 'In 2004, for the first time ever, LGBT-specific information was distributed to, and accepted by, schools nationwide. We sent a 10-page booklet and poster about LGBT youth awareness and affirmation to every post-primary school in the country.' BeLonG To also provides training to Social, Personal and Health Education teachers on working with LGBT youth and will be launching a 'Stop Homophobic Bullying in School' campaign and website in September 2006.

It was also pointed out that the responsibility for changing attitudes and providing support to young GLB individuals also lies with parents and that parents need to be supported in changing their attitudes as well.

There is also the issue of the Church's attitude towards homosexuality. Petra says that as a Christian who believes in living a true and transparent life, she experienced support, a sense of community and a sense of belonging within the Church for a long period of time. Since the revelation that she is homosexual, some people in the Church have stayed in contact with her, but the vast majority have shunned her. 'You do experience a sense of loneliness, but my faith and relationship with God hasn't changed. It takes a strong person to know what to do.'

Representations by organisations in Ireland in 2005, followed by a submission by BeLonG To in response to young people presenting to them with suicidal ideation, resulted in the inclusion of the GLB and transgender communities in the HSE's strategy document *Reach Out: National Strategy for Action on Suicide Prevention 2005–2014.* They were included as one of the marginalized groups which need to be looked at in terms of risk of vulnerability to suicidal behaviour. The recommended action going forward is to 'determine the risk of engaging in suicidal behaviour associated with belonging to a marginalised group, and to review the available services and support agencies for marginalised groups.' Based on the learnings from this first action, the second recommended action is to 'develop services, supports and information/education resources to improve mental health and well-being and reduce any increased risk of suicidal behaviour among marginalised people, in consultation with members of marginalised groups.'

Suicide and the Traveller Community

In the course of my research for this book on suicide, I interviewed a number of people who worked with bereavement organisations; they mentioned that they had come across members of the Traveller community who had been bereaved by suicide.

As the Traveller community accounts for such a small proportion of the entire population, 0.6 per cent, the mention of Traveller suicide on more than one occasion indicated that suicide was potentially a big issue in this community. I approached Pavee Point, who, along with a number of other organisations working with the Traveller community, were organising a Traveller Suicide Prevention Seminar. They explained that there are no official statistics available for the level of suicide within this community and it has not yet been established whether it is a particular problem. However, since September 2004, a number of Traveller organisations have been coming together to explore the issue of suicide within the Traveller community. Director of Pavee Point, Ronnie Fay, says there was concern at the perceived increase in Traveller suicide 'and [we] felt there was a need to prioritise this issue in our work and also to develop culturally appropriate responses to it'.

Ronnie told the seminar that, while suicide among the Traveller community shared similarities, in causality, with other suicides, there were also differences.

Although there are no proper statistics available for suicidal behaviour in Travellers, suicide in the Traveller community was, until relatively recently, considered to be less common than in the general population. Anecdotal evidence indicates an increase in suicide over the past 5–10 years, especially among young Traveller men. There is general agreement that there has, in the past, been a reluctance to talk about suicide within the Traveller community, but this is starting to change and some families affected by suicide are now more open to discussing it.

As the needs of marginalised ethnic communities are different from those of the community at large, it is seen as important to develop Traveller-specific training, research and clinical services. Speaking at the Traveller Suicide Prevention Seminar, child and adolescent psychologist Helen Keeley acknowledged that certain recent changes have occurred in Traveller culture, similar to those experienced in other cultures, which have resulted in a loss of role identity and traditional values. 'If a culture gives order and meaning to life experiences, then the dismantling of that culture may result in a disordered and meaningless world.' This may create a culture in which suicide flourishes.

The Traveller community faces a huge number of unique pressures that members of the settled community will never face. According to Helen Keeley, acculturation (the erosion of culture and traditional roles and values) can pose a risk for suicide in marginalised communities. She cited the example of the Inuit population in Canada as the most striking example of this risk and also made reference to Native American acculturation. She says that acculturation in that community 'by means of western education; legislation; language barriers; lack of clear role identity and being moved from native lands to reservations contributed to the suicide problem'.

Suicide is a complex problem, however, and loss of culture cannot be considered the sole cause for the perceived rise in the suicide rate. Traveller-specific issues, such as discrimination, provide ongoing challenges. Travellers also face a number of issues that confront the settled community as well – such as the changing status of men in society. Dr John Connolly of the Irish Association of Suicidology points out that the traditional role of men in Irish society is changing and poor self-esteem among men can be related to the resulting diminishment of the macho image. There are also status pressures in the Traveller community that are specific to men. At the seminar organised by Pavee Point, representatives from Traveller organisations agreed that status was important to men in general and, in the case of Traveller men, their sense of worth was, in the past, derived from traditional Traveller economic activities, such as tin-smithing. The stereotypical macho role of men seems to be even more pronounced in the Traveller community and this stands out as an issue because, as a result of that macho role, men are not seeking the help they need. It was pointed out at one of the workshops at the Traveller Suicide Prevention Seminar that, as Traveller men, they had to be tough growing up and crying was not allowed, making it harder for Traveller men to share their problems.

On the subject of whether there were any differences in the issues surrounding suicide in the settled community and the Traveller community, the seminar heard a number of opinions on how discrimination against the Traveller community was perceived to affect their well-being. There was a feeling that mistrust of the health services resulted in a low take-up of these services by the Traveller community and there was also a feeling that some GPs were not examining or treating Travellers properly. Identity issues for Travellers and the challenges to their value systems and their way of life are seen as specific factors that may contribute to suicide. The issue of shame is also very strong in the Traveller community and the effort to keep up appearances can put individuals under great pressure.

Since suicide was decriminalised in Ireland in 1993, there has been extensive work to reduce the stigma surrounding it. While there has been huge progress among the general population, in reducing that stigma and raising awareness around the problem, a huge stigma is still attached to suicide in the Traveller community. It was pointed out at the seminar that in order to develop a culturally appropriate response to suicide, people have to be able to actually say the word 'suicide', which many are afraid to do. There was a feeling among those gathered that this would help to take away the fear and shame around the issue.

There was general agreement at the seminar that the stigma around mental health issues in the Traveller community also needs to be challenged. Some Travellers see depression as being 'mad' and it was suggested that work needs to be done around these attitudes. It was noted at the seminar that Travellers are less likely to access counselling and therapeutic services in the early stages of a mental health problem and are more likely to engage such services only when the problem has become severe; this may be because Travellers do not feel comfortable or understood by settled therapists. Representatives of Traveller organisations who attended the seminar felt that services, such as counselling and other mental health services, are not Traveller-appropriate; this opinion was based on experiences of bringing Travellers to such services and finding that they were not suitable or appropriate to their needs or comfort levels.

As in the settled community, the stigma surrounding suicide has prevented the issue from coming to the fore and being tackled head on in the Traveller community. The stigma appears to be even stronger in the Traveller community and, with the perceived significant rise in suicide, movement is underway to find out more about it.

There are still no official figures available for the level of suicide in the Traveller community. The Traveller Suicide Prevention Seminar was a first step towards a serious consideration of the problem and towards assessment of whether the levels have increased. There was agreement at the seminar that carrying out research into the extent of the problem is a critical step forward, as is developing culturally appropriate counselling services for the Traveller community.

Nuala Whelan: Finding Happiness after Being Bereaved

It's shortly after 6.30 pm when I arrive at Nuala Whelan's house to have a chat with her about her life since the loss of her husband, John. Just over six years have passed since he died by suicide in 1999. She brings me into the kitchen where two of her sons, 16-year-old Eoin and 12-year-old Conor are finishing dinner at the kitchen table. They stand up and shake hands as Nuala introduces us. Nineteen-year-old Brendan walks in at that moment and says hello. The eldest of her eight children, 24-year-old Emma. is at her house in Wicklow, 23-year-old Derek lives in London, while Anne-Marie (21) is out, Siobhán (20) is at work and 14-year-old Edwin is at a football match. Nuala goes over to make tea, while Eoin brings his plate over to the dishwasher, double-checking that the dishes inside are not clean. Nuala invites me into the sitting-room for a chat, just in time to stop Eoin, who was slipping in to watch TV. Eoin grins, not a bother on him, and leaves us to it, only to pop in a little while later to offer us a cup of tea.

This is a family that has pulled together following the traumatic loss of a father and husband through suicide. After only minutes in their company, you can sense that they really look after each other and are very thoughtful and deeply conscious of the feelings of other people, because they've been through it all: they have been through the trauma of losing a beloved family member to suicide. Though Nuala still misses her husband and the children their father, the family has managed to move on with their lives and create a new normality.

'You never get over it, there's always something that will knock you back for a split second, but you learn to be happy.'

John's suicide at 41 years of age came completely out of the blue for Nuala. Although, looking back, she can say that her husband was probably depressed in the time leading up to his death, she certainly did not believe he had reached such a low ebb. The day he died was Monday, 19 July 1999. That morning John told his wife that he was taking the day off work as he wanted to go and talk to a member of his family. She heard him ring work and say he would not be coming in that day, but would be back to work the following day. He kissed Nuala goodbye and gave his daughter Emma a lift to work.

Nuala went to work herself and arrived back home at about 3 o'clock. She waited for John to come home but there was no sign of him. As the evening wore on, she began to get worried but couldn't contact him as he didn't have a mobile phone. He had never gone off like this before; however, Nuala felt he needed some time for himself and had gone off to do some thinking. The children weren't worried as their Dad worked shifts as a postal clerk and often worked nights, so they assumed that that was where he was. Nuala stayed up all Monday night, but John didn't turn up. The next day was her daughter Emma's 18th birthday, so for her sake, Nuala let on everything was rosy. That evening, they had dinner and a birthday cake and the children were none the wiser as to their father's absence.

At the time, the family was looking after two children from Chernobyl and after dinner, Emma decided to bring them up to visit her boyfriend's mother. Nuala rang her husband's workplace to see if her husband had turned up at work – he hadn't and she realised something was up. It was totally uncharacteristic of John to go away like that and not even get in touch.

Now feeling terrified about her husband's absence, she decided to ring her husband's sister to see if she had heard anything from him. 'I explained he had been missing since Monday morning.' His sister hadn't heard from him and Nuala wondered whether John may have gone to his old family home in Barna Choille in Sandyford, which now lay empty. He was very fond of the house and would often go up there. His sister came over to collect Nuala. They decided to contact John's other sister, who lived in Wicklow, and she started to make her way up to the house in Barna Choille as well.

When Nuala arrived at the house, she saw John's car outside and they went to search for him. When she got to the shed in the garden and put her hand on the door to open it, a neighbour stopped her in her tracks by shouting at her. Nuala's first thought was that the man was shouting at them for trespassing, but she soon learned that it was a lot more serious. John's sister and his brother-in-law had got there before them and had already been into the shed, where they had found John hanging. John's brother-in-law had sent the neighbour up to warn them.

Completely stunned, Nuala went up to a neighbour's house while the police and fire brigade arrived. Nuala says her immediate reaction on learning of her husband's death was to get home to the children. The neighbour's house was up a country road, however, and the fire brigade and ambulance were blocking the road, so Nuala couldn't leave until they had moved.

'My first instinct was just to go home. I just wanted to get home to the kids.' Nuala contacted her sister to tell her what had happened and she asked her to inform the five older children of their father's death. 'I insisted the children be told. I had always told my children not to tell lies and [I] didn't want to lie to them. I wanted to tell the younger ones myself. All I could think was *I have to get to the kids and how will I tell the younger ones?*'

After about an hour, the emergency services moved off and Nuala was able to go home. When she arrived back, she took the three smaller ones into her bedroom – they were aged six, eight and ten and told them that their daddy had passed away. 'I told them that he had chosen to go to heaven.' Eight-year-old Edwin, who had always been his father's shadow, was devastated. 'Edwin was always in the shed with his father when he was working with wood. He was always tidying up his dad's tools.' Ten-year-old Eoin was also devastated by the news; meanwhile, the baby of the family, Conor, who was only six, had no real concept of what had happened and though he cried, Nuala feels that that was really a reaction to the other children crying.

At 11.30 that evening the family received a call from the hospital to ask if they wanted to come and see John. 'I didn't want to see him, but the five older ones did.' John was identified by his brother-in-law and then Siobháin, Brendan, Anne-Marie, Derek and Emma went down to see him. When they got back from the hospital, they told their mother that John looked just like he was sleeping. Brendan asked if he could go straight to bed, while the others sat around talking about it with their cousins, who had come over to offer their support.

Nuala, who hadn't slept for the last couple of nights while John had been missing, was exhausted, but she realised that with eight young children to look after, their welfare was her immediate concern and she could not go to pieces. 'I think I switched off at the time. I functioned for the sake of the children. There was no point in dwelling on what I was going through. I was very careful not to take a drink or tablets – I was afraid I'd get dependant. I had eight children who had just lost their daddy and they needed me to be strong.'

The children took care of their father's funeral. Nuala sat them down at the kitchen table for a family meeting and was happy for them to look after it – she just reminded them to do it with decency and respect. 'The funeral gave the children a sense of letting go. Each of the children had their own job to do. They got great help and support from their school.' Although the funeral was very well-organised, Nuala couldn't help but wonder did her husband not see how many people loved and cared about him while he was alive.

The fact that John had died by suicide was particularly hard for the family. 'From the day John died, I lost my husband and my best friend and the children lost their father. With natural causes, you could say it was God's will, but suicide is very difficult to come to terms with. He was a very good man – he wasn't into drugs or drink. Overnight, I went from Nuala, the mother and wife, to Nuala, the mother, widow and provider. Suddenly, every decision I made had to be done alone. I used to have John, but now the unit was dismantled and I had to start from scratch.' From the very beginning of their life without John,

Nuala was very open with her children. 'I told them that I may make mistakes.'

Although Nuala had worked part-time before John's suicide, he had been the main provider and suddenly she was left with his last wage packet to look after the whole family. Luckily, they had always managed their finances well and apart from their mortgage, they owed just £4.50 to the bank. 'We never had a holiday and rarely went out. This was the sacrifice we made for a big family. Once the children were happy and healthy, we were happy.'

Although they had quite a small mortgage, Nuala did not have access to John's life insurance until after the inquest took place. 'I had a letter from the Coroner's Court but no death certificate and the insurance company wanted the official death certificate.' Nuala couldn't pay the mortgage during the seven-month wait for the inquest, but continued to receive letters from the financial institution looking for payments. She wrote to them to say she was awaiting the inquest, but they said there was nothing they could do and the letters continued to come. This didn't make life any easier and Nuala says she still dreads other official letters coming for John owing to glitches in the system. 'A tax form arrived for him this year and he's now six years dead. None had arrived last year or the year before.'

Nuala had to go and queue at the social welfare office for the first time in her life just two weeks after John had died to get something to tide her over until her widow's pension came through. She eventually received a widow's pension and half of John's pension to look after her family. Because these amounted to a set figure, Nuala did not receive state benefits. It was tough considering that she had eight children to put through school and further education.

The year after John's death, Nuala received a letter from the social welfare office saying she might be entitled to a back-to-school allowance for the children, but when she went to check it out, it turned out that her widow's pension, along with half of John's pension, put her £4 over the limit, so she got nothing at all. Before John's death, Nuala had worked part-time. They had a system in place – John would look after the children until Nuala came in and then he would go to work, but after he died, Nuala had to give up work. Although finances weren't easy, Nuala had to manage with what she was given and she did.

Physically providing for the children was Nuala's immediate concern, but she knew they would also have to deal with the emotional trauma of losing their father to suicide sooner rather than later. 'I thought it was better to go through it now than have to deal with it years later.' Her brother gave her a contact number for a counsellor in Bray, Co. Wicklow who ran groups for families bereaved by suicide. Sr Sheila O'Kelly, Director of the Wicklow Suicide Bereavement Support in Bray, recommended that the younger children participate in the Rainbows Programme. Rainbows is specially designed for children, or young adults up to the age of 16, who lose a parent through death or separation. Through drawing and games, a counsellor worked with the three younger children. The counsellor actually called to the house to work with them and Nuala says it was very effective. 'They were asked to draw pictures, for example, of how they saw their daddy's funeral and they seemed happy with the programme.'

At this point, the younger children did not realise that their father's death was through suicide and Nuala decided it was time to tell them. 'Edwin was only eight at the time and he wanted to know how his father had killed himself – he was so young I felt it was too severe, so I told him the inquest hadn't been held yet. I wouldn't lie to him and when he asked a couple of years later, I told him how his dad had died.' Nuala was curious as to why Edwin wanted to know about how his dad had taken his life and asked him about it. He told her that whenever he told any of his friends that his Dad had taken his life, they always asked how it had happened.

Nuala was afraid of the effect that the knowledge would have on the younger ones. 'I never slept that night, thinking the kids would be haunted for the rest of their lives.' In fact, telling the younger ones that John had died by suicide resulted in a huge change in the atmosphere in the house – for the better. Up until that point, the older ones had been protecting the younger ones from the truth, literally shadowing them and if any guest alluded to the fact, the older ones would try to cover it up. 'People would walk in and say, "God Nuala, why did he do it?" and then suddenly go silent and not mention it again.' Ultimately, it meant that the older ones weren't moving on and coping with their grief; by letting the rest of the children know, the environment in the house lightened considerably. 'It was as if a weight was lifted.'

With the younger ones enrolled in Rainbows, Nuala turned to the three teenage girls: Emma, Anne-Marie and Siobhán. 'We went out to Sr Sheila in October. I told the girls I knew nothing about the programme, but not to knock it until they tried it. I said it might help.' Emma and Siobhán went to just one session, but Anne-Marie continued to go and her brother Derek then joined the programme as well. Later, Emma went for one-to-one counselling. Nuala understood that everyone had their own way of dealing with their grief and let them choose the path they wished.

She would often sit them down around the large kitchen table for what she refers to as a 'family meeting'. 'I'd say to them that we were all in the same boat and we're all here to help each other. They were never made feel guilty for not pulling their weight when they were having a bad day. Something as traumatic as suicide can make or break a family.'

Some of the children would talk about their father and his death, some wouldn't. The family felt very little anger towards him for taking his life. 'It wasn't a doom and gloom scenario. This happened to us, but we had to deal with it. I told them we had to go out of the house, to the other side of the gate and get on with living. We couldn't sit and dwell on it.' Nuala herself feels that she was able to cope so well because she followed her gut instinct, which told her she had to get the children through this. Her philosophy was to live for the day and not even think of next week. 'I put everything in limbo for myself until two years after John died, until I knew the children were safe. I wouldn't even look at that side until I knew the kids were okay.'

That's not to say that Nuala didn't get annoyed and frustrated with the challenges of the outside world. The times that were particularly difficult included the first anniversary of John's death, their first Christmas without him only five months after he had died, and any family celebration at which a father would normally play a crucial role. That first Christmas was full of sadness and tears, but Nuala did not want to ignore the fact that Christmas was happening. 'Conor still expected Santa Claus to come. We had to function. Why ruin Christmas for the kids?' Since then, Nuala makes sure to play a Christmas CD starting in November and they always put a lighted candle in front of John's photo on Christmas Eve. Although some people didn't think it was a good idea, Nuala took the children to Butlin's fun-park on the first anniversary of John's death, visiting his grave later that evening. 'What was the point in sitting around the house bawling and whinging? I told the children for every tear we cried, I wanted to see a bucket of laughter.'

'I've never been angry with John. I never looked upon it as "I've been left with eight children" rather "we have eight children". Nobody's perfect in this world, but I think he has lost out big time.' They had been married for eighteen and a half years. Nuala doesn't feel John ever wanted to leave her and the children, but thinks he must have had some type of personal battle inside him. She had seen no sign that he had planned to take his life. They had a good relationship and John would often describe their marriage as a sense of humour – he being the sense and Nuala the humour. 'He was easy-going, nothing would rile him. He was good-natured. We talked about everything, we had no secrets.' With eight children, they generally only went out when there was a specific party or a wedding on. 'He was there for the children's births, he changed their nappies. He was involved with the Board of Management in the children's school – I was involved with the youth club and we always helped each other out.'

John also had a love of woodcarving and he and Nuala had built most of an extension to the house. John would also go away for a weekend with work to play pitch and putt, which he really enjoyed, and even though he was only away for the weekend, he'd always bring things back for the children. 'He was always doing stuff for me and the kids and would buy me flowers every week. The children would play us off each other – if I said no, they'd go and ask him.'

Nuala is very open when she talks about John. She doesn't hesitate to answer any question I put to her. She hopes that the story of how she coped and learned to be happy will help others in similar situations. John's death is a fact of life she can't change and, as we talk, she is a picture of strength and, indeed, normality. She is able to laugh when there is a funny moment. I ask her if she planned to have so many children and she jokes, 'I had always wanted loads of kids. I will look after kids and old people and the people in between can feck off!'

'[John] had promised the children that if he won the Lotto or won on prize bonds, he'd bring them to Florida, to Disneyland.' The year after John died, Nuala did manage to bring them to Disneyland. 'It was the best thing I could have done.'

John didn't have a drink or drugs problem – his father had died, but that was 18 years before and it seemed unlikely that this was a key factor in his suicide. He came from a large family, one of two brothers and four sisters. He missed his mother, whom he was very close to, when she moved to Co. Kerry, but otherwise everything seemed fine. He had no history of depression. He was very attached to the house where he had grown up in Barna Choille in Sandyford, and he was nostalgic about his youth, bringing the children to places where he used to go. 'My personal feeling is that he somehow backed himself into a corner.'

We take a break to avail of the kind offer of tea from Eoin and I comment on how good the children are. She laughs and tells me that she's trained them well. 'I always say the woman who gets my boys will be very lucky.' Throughout our discussion, we have the company of the family dog, Coby, who jumps up and gets us to open the door every time he hears one of the children or their friends come or go.

Nuala moves on to the experience of John's inquest, which caused a lot of anguish for her. It looked like the inquest was going to take place a few days before their first Christmas without John. Daughter Emma went to the Garda station to check when the inquest would be and asked the Garda to contact her mother. Nuala was at home in tears, worried that it would land upon her over Christmas. She received a call from the Garda to say that the inquest would be on the 21 December and was asked if the timing would be a problem.

Although Nuala had enough to cope with to try and get through their first Christmas without John, she felt that by dealing with it in December, they could start the new year afresh, with some closure, so she decided to go ahead. 'I was left in limbo until the inquest took place – I couldn't even sort my mortgage out without a death certificate for John and this was all adding to my grief.' Owing to administrative delays, the inquest did not go ahead on the date in question. Nuala was very angry because she wasn't informed and had to call the Coroner's Court and the Garda station to find out what was going on.

She didn't hear anything further until mid-January. Eventually, it went ahead on the 23 January. Although she had psyched herself up for the experience, she still found it intimidating. 'I was asked to stand up and I had to shout from one end of the court to the other end, as the room was so large.' The verdict returned was suicide. Nuala was unhappy that the death certificate she would now have to use for all official business stated very clearly that the cause of John's death was asphyxiation by hanging, suicide. This was visible to everyone she had to show it to, even when she was sorting out passports for the children. Even with John's death certificate, Nuala still had difficulties transferring their car into her name, and she had to go to the Garda station to get further official confirmation.

The time when the loss of John really hit Nuala was when her own father died. 'When my father died, it opened up old wounds. I wasn't with John when he died and I wondered what way did he go; was he crying? Looking for us? I had to face the reality.' Luckily, Nuala had the support of her older children and was able to discuss it with them. 'I still cry with them. Just after Father's Day, I was on the phone to Derek in England and the two of us were bawling on the phone. Derek had done a sponsored cycle for charity and his daddy wasn't there to be proud.'

'I miss John most when something good happens. The bad stuff I can cope with, but I missed him when Anne-Marie was called to the bar and at graduations and 21st birthdays.' There are so many occasions when the children really miss their father. They have all done really well and would love to have their father there for the proud moments. Emma, the eldest, is now 24. She had just finished her Leaving Certificate when her father died and she went on to do a Diploma in Interior Design. She has now bought her own house in Roundwood in Co. Wicklow, where she lives with her boyfriend of seven years. She passed her driving test and travels up and down to her job in a shop in Nutgrove. Her mum often goes down to visit Emma in her new house, the inside of which displays her skill for interior design. When Emma goes away on holidays, Nuala often brings the younger boys down for a couple of days. 'Emma's content,' her Mum smiles.

Derek, who is 23, has now moved to Canary Wharf in London to work in a top job in IT. 'He was head-hunted,' Nuala says proudly. 'He got first place in his year in UCD two years running. He was also very involved in the UCD boxing club.' Nuala is delighted for him as he had his heart set on this job and had worked very hard. He even got a Millenium scholarship from Bank of Ireland through his secondary school. Nuala has been over to visit him. 'He sent me a ticket for my Mother's Day present. He loves it over there and has settled in really well – he still comes home regularly to visit us.'

Twenty-one year old Anne-Marie has just qualified as a barrister with the Kings Inns. She, too, worked very hard to achieve her success and also received a Millenium scholarship through her school. 'We made history with two students from the one school getting a Millenium Scholarship,' smiles Nuala.

Siobháin, who is 20, is in her fourth year of nursing, which she loves. As we chat, Siobháin arrives home and pops in to say hello before going into the kitchen to talk to her siblings and her boyfriend, who has dropped over.

Nineteen-year-old Brendan is starting his third year of architecture in UCD, which he loves. 'That's another record,' laughs

Nuala. 'Four children from the same family going to UCD, one after the other – that's a record in UCD.'

Sixteen-year-old Eoin is starting his Leaving Cert year. He likes school and got the top results in the school in his Junior Cert exams. I remark on how well all of the children have done academically and Nuala insists she never pushed them, but always had a policy in the house that homework was to be done straight away. Once that was done and dusted, they were allowed to do what they wanted.

Edwin is 14 and is just starting his Junior Cert year, but he 'hates school with a vengeance'. Nuala says he is extremely helpful and willing to assist in school because it gets him out of class! 'He gets good grades, but I think he'll end up doing something manual. He is very into sports, especially football.' Indeed, Edwin is at a football match while we talk about him, and as luck would have it, he walks in the door a few moments later. He says hello and then turns to tell his mum that they won their match. He chats with his Mum about leagues and further games and I gather that the result bodes well for the future of the team.

Twelve-year-old Conor is the baby of the family. He is just starting second year in secondary school. He loves school and has already been put ahead a year. 'He is a sponge for knowledge and loves reading.'

The way the family has got on with their lives despite all the pain is very encouraging and Nuala always makes herself available to lend a listening ear to other people who have been bereaved by suicide. 'I tell them there's no magic wand, no formula to make it all better, but never be afraid to try to live with it. You never get over it but you learn to be happy, it becomes a norm.' John is missed terribly by the whole family. 'We talk about him every day. We go to his grave regularly and when we are out in the garden, the children are always saying, "Daddy used to do this or that", but his death is never taboo.'

Nuala wonders if John had just been able to get past the moment he was in when he took his life, would he still have chosen to do what he did. She knows he wouldn't have liked to see the sorrow caused to her and the children, but still she doesn't see the point in continuing to ask *Why?* She recalls how friends and family would walk in and always ask that question, 'Why did he do it?', even six months afterwards. 'It got to the point where I told the kids, I don't ever want to hear *Why?* again.' The children took her at her word to the point that, a while later, when Nuala was teaching the children to bake and they said, ' "that word we're not allowed use" do you mix the butter and flour together?!'

She says you have to be able to laugh at the funny side of things, even when things feel like they should be at their most serious. She recalls a moment just after John was laid out and they had gone in to see him in the morgue. 'John always worked in these open-toe sandals, which we called "Jaysiz sandals". He was to be laid out wearing them. The children went in to see him in twos. I was with Edwin and Brendan when we went into the mortuary. Edwin kept tapping me because he was excited about seeing his Daddy's name on the lid of the coffin. Brendan and Edwin were making signals to each other as they walked around their father's body. They were nodding at his feet and then asked me, "Can we look at his feet?" I said "yes" and they lifted the sheet at his feet. Brendan stared with a look of utter disgust, meanwhile, Edwin was laughing and they both exclaimed in unison, "He's no Jayzis sandals!" There was no way they were letting him go to heaven without them on! And the search for the sandals began!'

Nuala always makes herself available to talk to other families who are going through what she did: 'Everyone is an individual and a multitude of different things work for different people who are grieving. Suicide is not normal, so the grief road is not normal.' Drawing on her personal experience, Nuala's advice to any parent with young children who has to cope with the death of the other parent is to remember that children are different to adults. She doesn't believe in telling the story as you would to an older person: 'A 10-year-old can't think like an adult. I always asked them was there anything they wanted to know and assured them they could always ask me.' She feels her children have come out of the whole experience much more aware of people's pain. They always try and help others. 'When one of the children's friend's dad died, he talked about their crying and said, "I know what they're going through." They see that their daddy's death was his choice and we have to live by his choice.'

It is still difficult as the family is always labelled. 'They are the kids of the father who walked away and killed himself. You feel you have to justify the person who died when it's by suicide – that's the hardest part.' Still, no matter what happens, life does go on. 'At the time when John died, someone said "such and such is happening next month" and I thought how will I ever get through just this week?' But that week came and the one after it and the one after that. 'I've never believed in wasting time. Life is for living. Life is not a dress rehearsal.'

Suicide and Depression

Up to 90 per cent of all suicides are associated with mental illness and, according to Sandra Hogan from Aware, about 80 per cent of all suicides can be traced back to depression. Hence, the recognition and effective treatment of depression is key to an effective suicide prevention strategy.

Despite the link between suicide and mental illness, experts maintain that it is dangerous to explain suicide as simply a result of mental illness. Suicide is related to a combination of factors, and root causes extend from biological to psychological ones, as well as to the environment in which people live. Aware states that, while mood disorders or some form of psychiatric illness may be necessary to explain suicide deaths, on their own they don't tell the whole story.

It is also vital to understand that, of the people who suffer from depression or other mental illness, only a small minority take their lives. The tragedy is that depression can often go undetected and untreated. Owing to the stigma associated with mental illness, people are often embarrassed to admit to themselves and to others that they may be suffering from depression. Men, especially, are reluctant to talk about it, seeing it as a weakness and a challenge to their traditional 'macho' image. The stigma has been reduced somewhat in recent years, owing to information campaigns carried out both in Ireland and internationally, and the knowledge that depression is a treatable illness that is becoming more widespread.

Suicide is a particularly big issue in people who suffer from undiagnosed depression, who, as a result, are not receiving treatment or support. Sandra says that if people who suffer from depression are not supported or don't understand the illness, they may feel there is no way out. 'Depression can be very isolating. People can feel like they are the only one in the world who feels the way they do. They might feel like nobody else understands what they're going through.' She says it is important to help prevent people from getting to the stage where they feel there is no way out.

One of the first steps in treating depression is recognising it as an illness and knowing the symptoms so that help can be sought. It is also important to acknowledge that anyone, irrespective of age, gender or background, can be affected by depression.

There are three main types of depression: reactive depression, which is an extension of the normal upset feelings that can be brought about by negative life events, such as the death of someone close, the break-up of a relationship or the loss of a job; the second type of depression is uni-polar, also known as endogenous depression, which is primarily biological or inherited, but which can be brought on by disappointment or loss; the third type of depression is bipolar disorder, which has the same symptoms as uni-polar depression, but in which depressive episodes alternate with episodes of elation or mania.

RECOGNISING THE SYMPTOMS OF DEPRESSION (AWARE)

According to Aware, there are eight main symptoms of depression, summarised in the acronym FESTIVAL:

Feeling: depressed, sad, anxious or bored

Energy: tired, fatigued, everything an effort, slowed movements

Sleep: waking during the night or too early in the morning, oversleeping or trouble getting to sleep

Thinking: slow thinking, poor concentration, forgetful or indecisive

Interest: loss of interest in food, work, sex and life seems dull

Value: reduced sense of self-worth, low self-esteem or guilt

Aches: headaches, chest or other pains or palpitations without a physical basis

Live: not wanting to live, suicidal thoughts or thinking of death

Dr John Connolly of the Irish Association of Suicidology points out that the duration of these symptoms is important in distinguishing depression from ordinary unhappiness. 'Most clinicians would say that the symptoms must be present continuously for two weeks or more.'

According to Aware, depressive illness affects approximately 7 per cent of the Irish population and in excess of 300,000 Irish people are currently suffering from depression. Figures show that one in four people will suffer from a depressive episode at some point in their lives. In the past, as with suicide, there was a much greater stigma surrounding mental illness. While the stigma around mental illness has been significantly reduced in recent years, Aware says that we need to increase awareness and understanding of the illness further, so that depression can be diagnosed and people can receive the treatment and support that they need. Aware says depression must be recognised as an illness. 'A lot of people don't recognise depression as an illness.' A depressive disorder, if left untreated, can have a huge effect on an individual. Sandra Hogan says the illness can affect a person in a number of ways. 'It affects thinking, feeling, behaviour and [it] can be disabling.'

Aware points out that losses or setbacks in life such as relationship break-ups, bereavement, failure or social rejection can have a devastating effect on a person who is just about coping with depression. Also, they warn that many individuals who are depressed turn to alcohol or drugs to help them relax or sleep; however, these substances can frequently produce a profoundly depressive effect on a brain already experiencing the biochemical changes associated with depression.

Depression, if untreated, can lead to feelings of helplessness. Sandra explains that if a person is trying to cope with not being able to sleep, is preoccupied with losing their job or has a poor appetite, it can be extremely difficult to function. 'If they have a lack of motivation, it can be very difficult for them to carry on. Suicide is related to not having a positive connection with the future, thinking that things that are hard now are always going to remain the same.'

The symptoms of depression, when untreated, can have a huge impact on family members as well and this can make it even harder for an individual with the illness, when they see that others are worried about them.

On a positive note, people who suffer from depressive illnesses are extremely responsive to treatment. Better detection of depression and other mental illness is of crucial importance in reducing suicide among people with psychiatric illnesses. Counselling plays a very important role in promoting positive mental health and treating depression and suicidal behaviour. The Irish Association of Suicidology (IAS) says it is essential that policies and funding are put in place to develop comprehensive counselling services as part of the existing psychiatric services.

This is of particular relevance considering that many individuals who take their lives have been in touch with psychiatric services before their death. However, in the case of male suicides, they are much less likely to have been in touch with medical services prior to their deaths, a factor that indicates the importance of encouraging men to seek help when they are in crisis. With the notable number of people who engage in repeat deliberate self-harm or parasuicidal acts, it is clear that a system that offers the right counselling or treatment on an ongoing basis is required; the mental health services need the funding and staff to be in a position to do this.

A previous suicide attempt is a powerful indicator of suicide risk. Research shows that between 1 per cent and 3 per cent of individuals who attempt suicide will take their lives within 12 months of their attempt.

The IAS warns that sometimes people can be so depressed that they don't have the mental capacity to formulate a plan for suicide or have the physical ability to execute it. As they begin to recover, these abilities may return and this is why people may be at risk of suicide in the first week or two of treatment or hospitalisation. It has also sometimes been noted that some individuals who are depressed make an almost miraculous recovery although nothing has changed in their life situation. This false recovery may be a warning sign of impending suicide.

It is therefore advisable to keep an eye on people and continue to provide support and a listening ear, even when they appear to have recovered.

Aware says it is crucial to continue to raise awareness around depression and to let people know that there is help out there. Through information programmes, such as DAWN (Depression Awareness Week Nationwide), Aware seeks to continue to inform the public about depressive illness and promote further understanding of the symptoms, so that people do go and seek help. Aware highlights the issue at secondary school level through 'Beat the Blues' – an awareness programme delivered to students, which informs them about depression and explores support resources. Aware also brings people with depressive illness into the classrooms to talk to students and organises weekly support group meetings for people with depression and their families. Through the meetings, they aim to give information and emotional support to those who experience the illness and enable them to learn skills to deal with depression and build self-esteem. Aware's lo-call helpline, manned by trained volunteers, provides a listening ear to those in distress and to concerned family members.

As is frequently emphasised throughout the stories in this book, providing a listening ear can make a huge difference to people in crisis. If people are aware that there is support available, they are more likely to ask for the help they need.

For further information on depression, contact Aware on 01 661 7211 or go to www.aware.ie.

The Aware LoCall Helpline can be contacted on 1890 303302.

Reducing Suicide: The Australian Example and Dan Neville TD

Dan Neville TD is optimistic about reducing the level of suicide in Ireland in the future, especially among young people. Since 1997, there has been a 24 per cent decrease in the overall rate of suicide in Australia and Dan travelled to Canberra to learn more about the programmes they have put in place that have led to this reduction. He says similar programmes could and should be implemented in Ireland.

Dan was instrumental in bringing about the decriminalisation of suicide in Ireland in 1993. He brought the issue to the Senate and introduced a Private Members' Bill to decriminalise suicide. Though this bill was not passed, another was eventually and it was signed by President Mary Robinson on the 1 July 1993 – suicide was no longer a criminal offence in Ireland.

Shortly afterwards, Dan was contacted by professionals in the area of suicide research, including Dr John F. Connolly (present Secretary of the Irish Association of Suicidology [IAS]), Dr Patricia Casey and Michael Kelleher, who were all concerned about the levels of suicide in Ireland. They encouraged him to continue with work to help prevent suicide in Ireland and he attended a conference in Wexford on the issue. There were about 500 delegates at the conference and Dan brought some of the learnings into the Senate. Michael Kelleher proposed setting up a task force on suicide and Dan and Kelleher met with Minister for Justice, Michael Noonan, to formally propose a task force. A task force was set up, which reported directly to the International Association of Suicide Prevention. Michael Kelleher suggested setting up a similar national organisation for Ireland and in 1996, Dr John F. Connolly, Michael Kelleher and Dan Neville founded the IAS.

Dan believes that one of the key target areas for a suicide prevention strategy is the school system, as the whole population will attend school at some stage. 'We need to teach people what we have started.' Dan doesn't see educational pressures as a significant factor in suicide. Indeed, he points out that there is a higher level of suicide among people who drop out of the education system early, although the fact that they drop out could indicate that other problems already exist. The 2005 National Strategy on Suicide Prevention identifies as one of its objectives the establishment of a target to increase school attendance 'so that less young people fall through the protective net of continued education and training'.

Educating teachers about suicide and promoting positive mental health to children were recognised, at government level, as two important strategies by the 1998 National Task Force on Suicide. While some progress has been made and a number of schools have introduced Life Skills programmes since the 1998 Task Force, there is still a lot of work to be done and the 2005 National Strategy for Action on Suicide Prevention still lists promoting positive mental health and developing counselling services in all primary and secondary schools as goals.

When I spoke to Dan Neville at the launch of the strategy document, he told me that the recommendations for 2005–2014 were all very well, as long as they were put into action – his main concern was that they were very similar to the 1998 Task Force recommendations, many of which he felt had not been fully implemented, if at all. He is adamant that the budget for mental health services in Ireland is minimal and needs to be significantly increased.

Dan Neville points to the 32 per cent reduction in suicide among young people in Australia since 1997. That reduction has come about following several initiatives, including ones that directly target schools. In 2002 MindMatters was launched in secondary schools throughout Australia, placing mental health on the agenda. All Australian secondary schools were sent a MindMatters Resource Kit. There has been a massive response from schools to the MindMatters programme and huge participation in activities to learn more about suicide prevention. Evaluation has shown that 88 per cent of the 1,879 schools that participated in MindMatters professional development programme plan to implement what they have learned in the near future.

MindMatters is complemented by MindMatters Plus, which focuses on achieving better mental health outcomes for students with high support needs; this is achieved by using best practice prevention and early intervention programmes for mental health, educational and vocational programmes, as well as a range of supportive processes and strategies.

Australia also targets teachers and journalists at student level, to educate them on mental health promotion and early intervention and prevention of suicide.

Experts believe that talking is vital in tackling the suicide problem. There are 4.5 male suicides for every female suicide in Ireland and the fact that men find it more difficult to express their feelings could play a role in this over-representation of men. Indeed, Dan speaks highly of a campaign by Young Fine Gael called 'Talk', which was run in a number of third-level colleges. The aim of the campaign was to let people know that it's okay to talk when in crisis, and to let young men know that it's not unmanly to seek help.

In the course of my research for this book, a number of recommendations as to what could be done to target young people were frequently made by individuals very familiar with the subject of suicide. Darren Bolger's mother, Maureen, believes it is essential that young people learn about mental health issues at school and are provided with opportunities to talk about their problems. Since the loss of her 16-year-old son to suicide, she has established Teen-Line, so that young people can discuss their problems anonymously. Meanwhile, Pat Buckley, who lost two brothers to suicide, is determined to raise funds to build a youth centre where young people can feel secure and if need be, discuss anything bothering them. Bryan Walsh's brother, Tomas, told me that he would like to go into schools to share his personal story and highlight the importance of talking about problems that arise.

A number of the recommendations and the actions planned to target the problem of suicide in Ireland are very similar to Australian plans implemented to date. As mentioned earlier in this chapter, the overall rate of suicide in Australia has declined by 24 per cent since 1997. Even more inspiring, is the 32 per cent decline there in suicide among the under-25 age group in the same period. This last figure is of huge significance in an Irish context, especially as youth suicide rates in Ireland are the fifth highest in the European Union, according to the World Health Organisation.

Although some similar initiatives are planned for Ireland and in some cases have already begun, examples from Australia are very encouraging as they have progressed much further than Ireland and have significantly reduced their suicide rate.

In the spirit of Maureen Bolger's initiative for Teen-Line, the Kids Help Line (KHL) in Australia is a 24-hour national counselling service for children and young people aged 5–18.

KHL aims to assist young people in developing strategies and skills, so that they are in a position to more effectively manage their own lives. Professional counsellors are on board to deal with any problems and they will also refer young people on to appropriate organisations when appropriate. KHL has received a significant number of calls to date, indicating that young people welcome an opportunity to discuss their problems and to learn how to cope with life's challenges.

Taoiseach Bertie Ahern recognises that there is no single intervention or approach that will adequately challenge the problem of suicide in Ireland. Australia does not just target schools, but promotes activity across all aspects of society, in an effort to promote good mental health. Families are also directly encouraged to be aware of how to promote good mental health and to develop partnerships with schools through resource packs.

The work in Australia also includes increasing access to the internet for young people and a wealth of information pertaining to positive mental health is made available on the web. They also promote partnerships with business, government and community organisations to develop initiatives to inspire young people towards self-help and community involvement.

Key to a lot of the activity in Australia is letting people know about what is going on and how they can access services and information, while always ensuring that the reporting of mental health issues and suicide is done in a sensitive and responsible manner. The Australian Rotary Health Research Fund is working to increase the understanding of mental illness within local communities; one of the methods they use is making community service announcements for television and radio. Huge progress has been made in the five years since 2000 with announcements played by 65 television stations and 460 radio stations. The announcements are played on average 4,000 times per month.

The portrayal of suicide in the media poses a difficult challenge for journalists. The danger with media reporting of suicide is, if not done properly, not only can it cause severe pain and grief to the bereaved, but it can also lead to copycat suicides. Clearly, the role of the media is only one factor involved in some suicides. Suicide is complex and results from a series of different influences and issues in an individual's life. Copycat suicides can follow the suicide of a close friend or acquaintance, or they can follow a suicide learned about indirectly, through word of mouth or the media.

While the IAS agrees that the issue of suicide does merit reporting, they say it should not be glamorised. Nor should simplistic explanations for the cause of a suicide be given. They also recommend that contact details for support services should be included and advise against an over-emphasis on the deceased person's characteristics. Media are also advised to avoid giving detailed 'how to' descriptions of a suicide. (For further details on Media Guidelines, see the IAS website.)

In Australia, direct contact with the media regarding responsible reporting has been established through the Mindframe National Media Initiative, which seeks to influence the media industry to report mental illness and suicide issues responsibly, accurately and sensitively. Some of the work carried out by Mindframe includes the compilation of a media resource, which was issued to 1,536 media professionals and face-to-face briefings with media organisations to discuss issues of responsible reporting. SANE, an Australian charity that helps people affected by mental illness, established the StigmaWatch Program, which furthers the work of Mindframe by inviting the public to alert them to what they see as inaccurate or discriminatory reporting of mental illness. SANE will contact the relevant media organization to encourage them to report more accurately and sensitively in this area.

These are just some examples of the extensive programmes already in place in Australia. As evident in the examples above, there is great emphasis on targeting the general population in this approach to positive mental health. The success to date in Australia is the result of huge investment, in terms of time and research, and achievements like these cannot happen overnight. Similarly in Ireland, huge steps have been taken to prevent suicide since its decriminalisation in 1993 and the foundation of the IAS in 1996. For various reasons, Ireland was the last state in Western Europe to decriminalise suicide and was particularly late considering that suicide was decriminalised in the UK in 1961.

Despite the fact that suicide was decriminalised only very recently in Ireland and research into the subject was thus greatly hampered, the IAS, as well as countless voluntary organisations, have taken huge steps forward in raising awareness of the issue and putting pressure on the government to respond. We may not yet be at the same stage as Australia, but the examples of the initiatives that have worked over there are very similar to many suicide prevention initiatives that are already in place in Ireland. Indeed, the levels of suicide have gone down very slightly in Ireland since the rates peaked in 1998. The

Australian example and the work already underway in Ireland to date are, therefore, a cause for optimism. Dan Neville says that other countries have adopted aspects of the Australian model and achieved reductions in the level of suicide.

The Australian example focuses on very high awareness of and attention to positive mental health across all sectors of society. Indeed, as Dan Neville says in his 2004 *Suicide Awareness*, 'Suicide prevention is everybody's responsibility and the tide can only be turned by concerted, co-ordinated action by all parts of our society.'

Warning Signs of Suicide

1. Unexpected and sudden reduction in performance – at work, in their studies, in their family life.
2. Exploring ideas and themes of depression, death and suicide.
3. Talking about depression, death and suicide.
4. Changes in mood – emotional instability, swinging from bubbly to depressed.
5. Significant grief or stress – withdrawing from friends, family and society, watching TV but not really watching it.
6. Carelessness about appearance/personal hygiene.
7. Making jokes about suicide.
8. Religious despair – believing in religion and then losing faith.
9. Statements like 'I want to kill myself' have to be taken seriously.
10. Speaking of reunions with deceased people. 'I want to be with my partner/my mother'.
11. Drawings, illustrations or music about death or suicide, playing music about suicide.
12. Revisiting favourite places.
13. Giving away treasured possessions, such as football jerseys or a favourite CD.
14. Engaging in high-risk behaviour.
15. Feelings of helplessness and hopelessness – feeling trapped as if there's no way out, seeing no reason to live, having no sense of purpose in life.
16. Increased alcohol or drug use.
17. Anxiety, agitation, inability to sleep or sleeping all the time.
18. Saying things like 'people would be better off without me.'

Myths about Suicide (From the Irish Association of Suicidology)

1. *Those who talk about suicide are least likely to attempt it.* This is not true, about 80 per cent of those who take their own lives will have talked about it to some significant other in the few months beforehand.

2. *If someone is going to complete suicide they are going to do it and there is nothing you can do about it.* The majority of those who take their own lives are ambivalent about doing so until the end. Most people who complete suicide do not want to die, they just want to end their pain.

3. *You can get a good idea how serious someone is about a suicide attempt by looking at the method used.* This is not true. Most people have little awareness of the lethality of what they are doing. The seriousness of the attempt is not necessarily related to the seriousness of the intent.

4. *If someone has a history of making cries for help then they won't do it for real.* This is not true. The people at highest risk for suicide are those who have attempted it in the previous year.

5. *Only the clinically depressed make serious suicide attempts.* This is not true. People suffering from other forms of psychiatric illness and emotional distress are also at risk.

6. *A good pumping out in casualty will teach those who make silly gestures a good lesson they won't forget.* Attempted suicide should always be taken seriously. A person who has attempted to take their own life may choose a more certain method next time. It

is important that hospital staff, family and friends support the person in their recovery.

7. *Those with personality disorders attempt suicide to manipulate others.* This is a commonly held belief. Many a patient is alienated and an ideal opportunity for therapeutic intervention missed because of the reception they receive in some emergency departments.

8. *If someone is going to commit suicide, they will not tell anyone of their intentions and prepare well in advance.* This is not true. Many suicides are completed on impulse.

9. *Talking about suicide encourages it.* This is not true. Raising the issue of suicide with those who are depressed or distressed may open the door to therapeutic intervention.

10. *Suicide can be a blessed relief not just for the individual but for those surrounding him or her.* This is not true. Bereavement by suicide is a very heavy cross to bear; those bereaved by suicide have special needs and need special support. Bereavement by suicide is in itself a risk factor for suicide.

Bereaved by Suicide

Though death is a part of life, it is always very difficult to lose a loved one and come to terms with their loss. Losing someone to suicide is particularly hard, and the bereavement process is very different and unique. There are so many questions, especially *Why?* Added to this are feelings of anger. Loved ones can't understand why the person, who was supposed to care about them, visited such devastation upon the family. Sometimes, people push down these feelings of anger, but this anger must be dealt with as it can be very harmful.

Feelings of rejection are particularly common in those bereaved by suicide. Following the loss of a loved one, it is also common to sink into a state of depression. The journey through grief is long and difficult and no-one is prepared for this journey, especially when it is a result of a suicide. It is very difficult to accept the reality of the person's death, as can be seen in some of the stories in this book. Some of the families I spoke to told me that months and even years after the death of their loved one, they still expected to see the person's face among the crowd.

Often, by the time the reality of the death of a loved one hits a bereaved individual, much of the support network of friends and family, who were around in the aftermath of the death, have returned to their everyday lives in the belief that the bereaved person is okay; this can make the journey through grief all the more lonely.

Grief can even bring on physical symptoms such as sleeplessness or oversleeping, loss or gain of weight, tightness in the throat, an inability to concentrate and even headaches and stomach aches.

Then, there is the guilt, as loved ones wonder if they were there for the person, if they showed them that they loved them and question how they did not notice what was going on. Added to all of this pain is the stigma still associated with suicide, with some people (especially before suicide was decriminalised) actually hiding the reality of how their loved one died, which inevitably puts a much greater burden on the family. Furthermore, some families prefer to hide the truth from younger children, which adds to the tension in the home.

And then, of course, there's the Catholic Church. Parents wonder whether their son or daughter will go to hell for taking their lives, adding considerable mental torture to someone who is already grieving the tragic loss of a loved one through suicide. The Church has become much more sympathetic in recent years, indeed, a lot of the advice and support available for people bereaved by suicide is provided by members of the Catholic Church who have nothing but sympathy for those who have died by suicide and whole-hearted empathy for the tragically bereaved.

All of these painful factors are part of the journey through grief. Loss of someone through suicide will change you and your family. It is essential to understand the nature of grief and to maintain hope and determination that you will survive the loss.

SUICIDE AND THE JOURNEY THROUGH GRIEF

The presentation below, 'Suicide and the Journey through Grief' by Sr Kathleen Maguire PBVM. MA, provided great comfort to families bereaved by suicide at the STOP conference on suicide in 2005.

'There are probably many among you who are very qualified and familiar with the subject of grief. My talk will be in a reflective, sharing manner, in which I want to address those of you grieving the loss of a loved one by suicide. Death, especially a death by suicide, is difficult at any time. Probably the most painful and stressful experience we'll have in life is to be cut off from someone we love, who we won't see again in this world.'

Sr Kathleen told the conference of her own experiences of grief, to highlight her understanding and empathy with those gathered. 'We were 11 siblings in my family. There are just five of us left, out of a family of 13. Some died of long illness. Between the ages of 10 and 13, I lost my two-year-old brother and my mother died. All of these experiences of death have been horrific. Each had its own terrible pain. Sr Kathleen said, however, that the grief resulting from suicide is much harder. 'We've no doubt that there was something more difficult and painful when my niece's 48-year-old husband and my 21-year-old grandnephew died by suicide. I'll never forget it.'

Sr Kathleen spoke of how, during her personal experience of loss, she sometimes felt physically sick, such was the enormity of her grief. But, she pointed out, 'Grief is not an illness, it's an emotion. It is natural for us to grieve. Hundreds of millions of people die. At this moment, thousands of millions are grieving. But when it happens to us, we feel it has never happened before in the whole world. In a sense that is true – it's the first time for the individual. Grief is personal. Each time, it is as if it has never happened before. Grief is nature's way of healing a broken heart.'

Sr Kathleen told the bereaved that there is no getting around the terrible pain of losing a loved one who has decided to take his or her own life, though, down the line, people learn to cope with it.

BEREAVED BY SUICIDE – THE GRIEF PROCESS (SR KATHLEEN MAGUIRE, STOP CONFERENCE, 2005)

Shock and Denial: 'The first stage of grief is shock and denial. Everything inside us shouts, "No. This cannot be happening to me. Surely, my loved one is not gone. He/she will be back." We can sometimes act like robots, as if nothing is happening, as if it is all a bad dream. The shock protects us until we are able to deal with the reality of our loss.

Anger: 'Another thing that bothers us when somebody dies is the feeling of anger. "Why should this happen to me?" We are angry with priests, guards, psychologists, the hospital, friends, family members. We are angry with the deceased. When the reality of the death begins to dawn, the next reaction might well be outrage. Anger is a very natural stage of grief. But what do we do with our anger? We must be positive. We must do something, for example, walk, talk, run, pound a pillow. We must never be afraid to say that we feel angry – even to show our anger – within limits, of course! For God's sake, don't bottle it up! Talk to someone – a family member, a priest, whoever you are comfortable with. Anger is natural.

Guilt: 'We blame ourselves. A feeling within us, blaming ourselves for something we could have done. Guilt, especially when the death is by suicide, is very closely connected to blame. We blame ourselves for things we said and didn't say, and we feel guilty. You see, we very often hurt those we really love. Those we love, we often take for granted. We take liberties with them, not in a bad way, but we feel so comfortable with them, we don't think. We all do and say things that we regret afterwards. When a loved one dies before we get the opportunity to say we are sorry, then we can be in big trouble with our feelings. This stage of grief, especially when the death is by suicide, is very painful. The *if onlys* can go on and on and they can be very painful, especially at a time of suicide. There are two types of guilt, realistic guilt, which is what we feel when we've really deliberately done something to hurt or offend others. Then there is unrealistic guilt – the man who wouldn't let his son drive the brand new sports car because he was concerned for his safety. He saw his son starting up the car a few days later and told him to get out as he had been told not to drive it. The son went out the back of the house and took his life.

Bewilderment: 'There are times in grief when you become totally bewildered and feel lost. We keep asking ourselves Why, why, why? Sometimes, it's impulsive, like a bolt out of the blue. We ask ourselves why it happened. It could happen after a long illness, when someone couldn't take it anymore. There is a sense of relief, maybe in the above case – so we're totally bewildered. This bewilderment can bring around an awful feeling of depression. When someone dies, especially by suicide, we don't know what to do. If you know that someone has lost someone dear and they are very depressed, be careful to keep an eye on them – they may not talk about it.

Fear: 'As C.S. Lewis said, "No one told me that grief is so much like fear." We feel the need to be near loved ones.

Feelings of Shame and Blame, Total Rejection: 'It's difficult to believe that someone we loved and we believed loved us decided to end it all. People ask, "What do I do about this awful feeling?" They feel it will never end. I assure you it will come to an end and you will feel better. To begin healing, accept what has happened. "My loved one is dead. They decided to end their own life." Accepting reality will bring us hope, which, in turn, will bring us peace. This conference is to reach out to others in their grief. We have been through that pain … We need to help others through this pain.'

Sr Kathleen closed her presentation by reminding those gathered that loved ones would want them to get on with their lives. 'How many suicide notes have messages of love? Loved ones want us to live on, be happier and get on with our lives. I'd like to offer you that. Get on with your life. Only when we live like this will we be able to get on with our own grief.'

Speaking on the same evening, Rev. Dr Tony Byrne dispelled any fears of eternal damnation for those who have died by suicide. 'Anybody worried about their loved ones who died going to hell, have to get that out of their minds.' He reminded all gathered that suicide was decriminalised in 1993. 'For it to be a serious sin, it would need full consent and full knowledge. A person who dies by suicide could not possibly have full responsibility. Ninety per cent of all people who die by suicide have diminished responsibility.' He spoke of a man, whom he had saved twice, who had tried to kill himself. 'I asked him to please tell me what his mind was like at the time and he said, "The shutters of my mind closed down and I was in total darkness." How could anybody say he was responsible?'

According to *You Are Not Alone: Midlands Guide for Survivors in Managing the Aftermath of Suicide*, produced by the Midland Health Board, death by suicide is an overwhelming loss that can leave families and friends besieged by a range of emotions and many unanswered questions. The guide states that, while the pattern of grief is unique to individuals, many families experience similar reactions. While the big question when bereaved by suicide is *Why?*, they point out that it is not always possible to understand. 'What is important is to grieve and to come to a state of acceptance. While grieving never completely ends, the pain will soften over time' (*You Are Not Alone: Midlands Guide for Survivors in Managing the Aftermath of Suicide*).

The feelings of guilt described above by Sr Kathleen are common and natural. Grieving people need to accept that it was not their fault. Rev. Dr Byrne says suicide is 'a human act, which is self-inflicted, self-intentional, leading to a cessation of life'. He stresses how important it is that people who are grieving understand this. 'It's self-inflicted. Nobody else can be totally responsible for a suicide. We need to avoid getting into a complex that we can save the world. No matter what we do, people will try to kill themselves.' Parents may feel more guilt when their child takes his or her life as there is a widespread, but false, belief that if the victim had been loved enough and listened to enough, the suicide could and should have been prevented. This false belief comes from a lack of understanding and can cause considerable hurt and guilt to bereaved families.

It is vital for parents to realise that bad parenting does not cause suicide, any more than good parenting prevents it. People can be riddled with guilt, especially if a loved one takes his or her life after a row or an argument. It is vital for bereaved people to remember that arguments are a part of life and that the circumstances surrounding a suicide are many and complicated. If all arguments were to be followed by the suicide of one of the parties involved, there would be very few, if any, individuals alive in the world today.

The same is true of relationship break-ups. While intense guilt can be felt by a person who ends a relationship with an individual who then takes their lives, the explanation for the suicide is not that simple. Sr Kathleen says, 'Don't ever blame yourself for the death of another by suicide,' and advises that if feelings of guilt are very intense or if they go on too long, it is vitally important to talk to someone.

IF YOU HAVE LOST CHILDREN

Sr Sheila O'Kelly tells families who have lost children that it is important to remember the following:

You are a good person who has experienced a real tragedy.

You did the best you could. You are not to blame.

You loved your child in the best way you knew how.

You have a life worth living and more loving to do.

You have other people who need you and you need them.

You have a future and right now you have some rebuilding to do.

You are a suicide survivor. And you are not alone. Millions of people are suicide survivors.

Be patient with yourself. Recovering from grief takes time. Take one day, one hour at a time.

WHAT SHOULD I SAY TO THE FAMILY?

Inappropriate or tactless reactions to those bereaved by suicide can make the grief process more difficult. Now the stigma in Ireland has been significantly reduced, but, in the past, people were often reluctant to mention the word 'suicide' and sometimes avoided the bereaved family altogether, not knowing what to say. Below are guidelines from Sr Sheila O'Kelly of Bray Suicide Bereavement Support on what to say to those who have been bereaved by suicide.

Do say you are sorry about what has happened.

Do allow the bereaved to express their pain.

Do let genuine care and concern show and be felt.

Do reassure them that what they are feeling is normal.

Do show respect no matter what their story.

Do allow the person to be where they're at in their grief, not where you want them to be.

Do support their search for meaning.

Don't say that you know how they feel.

Don't push your religious beliefs or values on someone vulnerable.

Don't minimise their pain and don't support denial.

Don't let your discomfort with their tears come across to them.

Don't deny their guilt or encourage blame.

Don't avoid mentioning the deceased's name.

WHAT CAN I DO TO HELP MYSELF DEAL WITH THE BEREAVEMENT?

Know you can survive.

Know you may feel overwhelmed by your feelings; this is normal.

Anger and guilt are common responses. It's okay to express your anger.

Find a good listener.

Don't be afraid to cry.

Be patient with yourself and with others who may not understand.

Seek help and support.

HELPING A CHILD TO COPE WITH BEREAVEMENT AS A RESULT OF SUICIDE

Helping a child to cope with bereavement as a result of suicide provides a particular challenge for adults. Noel Sheehy highlighted at the IAS Conference on Suicide and Mental Health that the large increase in suicide in the UK and Ireland over the last three decades suggests that children are more likely to come across a suicide than their parents were during their childhood. He said that this can be a source of much anxiety and ambiguity for parents broaching the subject with their children. In some of the personal stories in this book, parents sometimes avoided telling younger children that suicide was the cause of a loved one's death, which, they point out, resulted in considerable tension in the home as everyone tried to cover up the truth to protect the younger children. The organisation Rainbows is geared towards helping children and adults who are grieving as a result of a death, divorce or any other painful transition in their families. Sr Sheila O'Kelly in Bray has found that the programme has worked very well for young children bereaved by suicide. A counsellor works with young children, using a workbook in which they can express themselves through games, exercises and drawing. Contact information for Rainbows can be found at the back of this book.

On the following page, are some guidelines, compiled by Jean Casey MIACP (See chapter 7) and presented at the April 2005 Bereavement Workshop, on how parents might discuss the suicide of a family member with young children.

1. Information about the suicide should be given in an honest and straightforward fashion. This strengthens trust between parent and child. Matter-of-fact information lessens the danger of children thinking that they may be responsible in some way for the death of a loved one.

2. Include them in the mourning process, allowing them to help in the funeral rituals.

3. Try not to allow the children to feel guilty. The extent of childish fantasy is impossible to gauge. Discussion can help.

4. Be prepared for anger. Children may blame the surviving adults for not preventing the suicide. Children may also suppress their anger towards the victim, because they don't want to upset the surviving adults. Parents need to encourage a family atmosphere which will permit open expression of these angry feelings. This will prevent the feelings from being turned inward and becoming self-destructive. Young people should also be encouraged to talk to trusted people outside the family.

5. Children need to be helped to anticipate the distorted thinking they are liable to encounter from classmates and others.

6. For children, certain dates take on great significance. Be prepared for this and go along with it.

7. Listen carefully to their questions, then, answer truthfully. Remain consistent in your truthful answers about the suicide.

8. Talk about the dead family member.

9. Teach your children to be selective about sharing the facts of the suicide with others.

10. Cry with them, show them that crying is an acceptable and natural release for grief.

11. Teach them that problems may frighten them, but let them know that all their feelings are normal, and to be expected. Having thoughts of wanting to die are also normal as long as they don't act on them.

Further Information

IRISH ASSOCIATION OF SUICIDOLOGY (IAS), St. Mary's Hospital, 16 New Antrim Street, Castlebar, County Mayo. Tel: (094) 9250858. Fax: (094) 9250859. Web: www.ias.ie .

AMERICAN ASSOCIATION OF SUICIDOLOGY, 5221 Wisconsin Avenue, NW, Washington, DC 20015. Tel: (202) 237-2280. Fax: (202) 237-2282. Web: www.suicidology.org

NATIONAL SUICIDE RESEARCH FOUNDATION, Perrott Avenue, College Road. Cork. Tel: (021) 4277499. Email: nsrf@iol.ie. Web: www.nsrf.org

Support Organisations

SAMARITANS. Tel: 1850 609090

AWARE, DEFEAT DEPRESSION, Head Office, 72 Lower Leeson Street, Dublin 2. Tel: (01) 661 7211. Fax: (01) 661 7217. Email: info@aware.ie. Web: www.aware.ie

RAINBOWS IRELAND LIMITED, Loreto Centre, Crumlin Road, Dublin 12. Tel: (01) 473 4175

ALCOHOLICS ANONYMOUS, 109 South Circular Road, Leonard's Corner, Dublin 8. Tel: (01) 4538998. Fax: (01) 453 7673. Email: ala@indigo.ie.

ISPCC HEAD OFFICE, 20 Molesworth Street, Dublin 2.Tel: (01) 679 4944. Email: ispcc@ispcc.ie

SCHIZOPHRENIA IRELAND, 38 Blessington Street, Dublin 7. Tel: (01) 860 1620. Email: info@sirl.ie. Web: www.sirl.ie

TEEN-LINE (ASSOCIATION FOR SUICIDE PREVENTION), 1 Parkhill Court, Kilnamanagh, Tallaght, Dublin 24. Tel: (01) 462 1933. Alternatively, contact Maureen on 085 7416019 or Eithne on 085 7417934. Email: eithnedunne@hotmail.com

A.B.C. ANTI BULLYING RESEARCH AND RESOURCE UNIT, Room 3125, Arts Building, Trinity College, Dublin 2. Tel: (01) 608 2573. Email lmcguire@tcd.ie. Web: www.abc.tcd.ie

MENTAL HEALTH IRELAND, Mensana House, 6 Adelaide Street, Dun Laoghaire, Co. Dublin. Tel: (01) 284 1166. Email: information@mentalhealthireland.ie. Web: www.mentalhealthireland.ie

DÓCHAS, The Oratory, Blanchardstown Centre, (Yellow Entrance). Tel: (01) 8200915 or 086 8806300

Bereavement Support

Console offers suicide bereavement support services and professional counselling nationwide. Ring the national freephone helpline for support in your local area. Console, Bereaved by Suicide Foundation, All Hallows College, Grace Park Road, Drumcondra, Dublin 9. Tel: (01) 857 4300. Helpline: 1800 201 890. Email: info@console.ie. Web: www.console.ie

National Suicide Bereavement Support Network, PO Box 1, Youghal, Co. Cork. Email: info@nsbsn.org. Web: www.nsbsn.org/index.htm

ANTRIM Belfast Cruse Bereavement Care, 10 College Green, Belfast. Tel: (028) 9023 2695/(028) 9043 4600. UK/N.I. Helpline: 0870 1671677. Web: www.crusebereavementcare.org.uk

CARLOW The Bereavement Counselling Service, Dublin, Carlow and Newbridge. For information on the range of services provided, contact Dublin Street, Baldoyle, Dublin 13. Tel: (01) 839 1766

CORK

Irish Friends of the Suicide Bereaved, The Planning Office, St. Finbarr's Hospital, Co. Cork. Tel: (021) 4136772

Let's Get Together Foundation, Midleton, Co. Cork. Tel: (021) 4636634. Fax: (021) 463 6634

Southern Health Board offer a bereavement support service, available at 087 2995913

DERRY Foyle Cruse Bereavement Care, 4 Dacre Terrace, Derry/Londonderry/Doire. Tel: (028) 71 262941. N.I./UK Helpline: 0870 1671677. Email: foylecruise@hotmail.com

DONEGAL Diocesan Pastoral Centre, Letterkenny offers a variety of services. Suicide bereavement support is available on the last Friday of the month. Contact: Sister Mary O' Donovan. Tel: (074) 9121853

DOWN Newry & Mourne Cruse Bereavement Care, 3 Edward Street, Newry, Co. Down. Tel: (028) 3025 2322. Email: cruse.newrymourne@talk21.com

DUBLIN

Solas, Bereavement Counselling for Children, Barnardos, Christchurch Square, Dublin 8.
Tel: (01) 473 2110
Tallaght Suicide Bereavement Support Group. Tallaght Hospital, Dublin, Tel: (01) 4142485

GALWAY Diocesan Pastoral Centre, Arus de Brun, Newtownsmith. Tel: (091) 565066 or contact Sr Marguerite Buckley on 087 6405239.

KERRY

Cluaiscint (Support for families and friends bereaved by suicide), St Brendan's Pastoral Centre, Upper Rock Road, Tralee, Co. Kerry. Tel: (066) 7125932

KILDARE

Bereavement Counselling Services, Newbridge Parish Centre, Station Road, Newbridge, Co.Kildare. Tel: (045) 433563

KILKENNY Bereavement Support Group, 27 Riverview, Kilkenny. Contact Mr Padraig Morrow on (056) 626421

LIMERICK Suicide Bereavement Support Network, Pastoral Centre, Denmark Street, Limerick. Tel: (061) 400133

LONGFORD Community Mental Health Centre, Dublin Rd, Longford (Co-ordinator, Ann Howard)

ROSCOMMON Boyle Suicide Bereavement Support Group, Family Centre, Boyle, Co. Roscommon. Contact Sr. Brigid Ward at (071) 9663000

TIPPERARY Living Links provides Outreach Support for suicide bereavement in North Tipperary. Tel: 087 969 3021

TYRONE

Omagh & Fermanagh Cruse Bereavement Care, Riverside House, Woodvale Avenue, Omagh. Tel: (028) 82 244414, 10.00–1.00 Monday to Friday, answering machine outside office hours.

WESTMEATH

Ring Rita Kelly on 086 8157320, fax on 0506 46747, or email at rita.kelly@mhb.ie.
Mullingar Suicide Bereavement Support Group, Bethany, Bishopsgate St, Mullingar. Tel: (044) 42746

WEXFORD HOPE Suicide Bereavement Support, Community Health Centre, Summerhill, Tel: (053) 23899

WICKLOW

Suicide Bereavement Support, Holy Redeemer Parish Centre, Bray (Sr Sheila O Kelly). Tel: (01) 2868413
Bereavement Counselling Services, Florence Road, Bray. Tel: 01 8391766, Mon–Fri, 9.15 to 1.00pm.

BIBLIOGRAPHY

Aware (Farren, Dr C.K. and Martin, Dr S.), *Aware Commissioned Report on Alcohol and Suicide: Interim Findings*, Dual Diagnosis Treatment Centre, St Patrick's Hospital, (Aware, 2004)

Aware, *Suicide in Ireland: A Global Perspective and a National Strategy* (Dublin: Aware Publications, 1998)

Aware, volume 18, issue 2, (Dublin: Aware Publications, 2005)

Byrne, Rev. Fr Tony; Maguire, Sr Kathleen; Byrne, Brendan; *Bullying in the Workplace, Home and School: Questions and Answers*, (Dublin: Blackhall Publishing, 2004)

Collins, Eoin and Dillon, Brian; Gay HIV Strategies in Conjunction with the Northern Area Health Board; *Strategies to Promote the Mental Health of Lesbians and Gay Men*, (Dublin: Nexus Research Co-operative Dublin, 2004)

Connolly, Dr John F. and Lester, David, *Suicide Rates in Irish Counties* and *Suicide Rates in Irish Counties: 10 Years Later*, Irish Journal Of Psychological Medicine 18(3):87–89, (Dublin, 2001)

Console, *Living with Suicide*, Console Publications, (1998).

Corcoran, P.; Reilly, M.; Salim, A.; Brennan, A.; Keeley, H. and Perry, I.J. 'Temporal Variation in Irish Suicide Rates', *Suicide and Life-Threatening Behavior* 34(4): 429-438, (2004)

Crowley, Philip; Kilroe, Jean; Burke Sara in conjunction with the Health Development Agency, *Youth Suicide Prevention Evidence Briefing*, Institute of Public Health in Ireland (2004).

Department of Health and Children, *Report of the National Task Force on Suicide*, (Stationery Office, 1998)

Farren, Dr C.K. and Martin, Dr S., *Aware Commissioned Report on Alcohol and Suicide: Interim Findings*, Dual Diagnosis Treatment Centre, St Patrick's Hospital, (Aware, 2004)

Foyle Search & Rescue; *Foyle Search & Rescue Information Booklet*, (Derry, 2004)

GMHP, *Gay Men's Health Project Annual Report*, (East Coast Area Health Board, 2003)

Health Service Executive, *You Are Not Alone: A Guide for Survivors in Managing the Aftermath of a Suicide.*

IAS, *Irish Association of Suicidology Newsletter*, (2004, 2005)

IAS, *Bullying and Suicide in Schools Proceedings of the Second National Conference* (2002)

IAS, *Alcohol, Substance Misuse & Suicidal Behaviour Conference Proceedings*, (2003)

IAS, *Schools Based Interventions in Crisis Management & Suicide Prevention, Conference Proceedings* (2004)

IAS, *Suicide – Human Tragedy – Global Responsibility: Second Annual Conference Proceedings* (1997)

IAS, *Suicide and Mental Health – What Counts? What's New? What Works? Proceedings of 6th Annual Conference* (2001)

IAS, *Suicide and Older People, Proceedings of the 8th Annual Conference* (2003)

Irish Prison Service, *Irish Prison Service Report 1999 and 2000*, (Dublin: The Stationery Office, 2002)

Irish Prison Service (2003). Report The Stationery Office

Irish Prison Service. Annual Report. The Stationery Office. (2002)

Maguire, Kathleen Sr. PBVM. MA., *Grief and Suicide*

National Educational Psychological Service. *Responding to Critical Incidents: Advice and Information Pack for Schools*

National Suicide Research Foundation (compiled by Paul Corcoran and Mark Kelly with valuable support and input from Ivan Perry, Eileen Williamson, Ella Arensman, Harry Comber, Colin Thunhurst, Irene Orchard, Helen Keeley), *National Parasuicide Registry Ireland Annual Report 2002*

Neville, Dan, *Suicide Awareness*, (IAS, 2004)

O'Mahony P. *Mountjoy Prisoners: A Sociological & Criminological Profile*, (Dublin: Stationery Office, 1997)

Oregon Resiliency Project, University of Oregon, *Recognizing and Understanding Depression in Children and Adolescents: A Handout for Parents*, (University of Oregon, 2003)

Oregon Resiliency Project, University of Oregon, *Youth and Adolescent Suicide: A Guide for Educators* (University of Oregon, 2003)

Health Service Executive, the National Suicide Review Group and Department of Health and Children, *Reach Out: National Strategy for Action on Suicide Prevention 2005–2014*, (Dublin: Health Service Executive, 2005)

Schizophrenia Ireland, Lucia Foundation. *Annual Report 2004*

Schizophrenia Ireland, Lucia Foundation, *Supporting Life: Suicide Prevention for Mental Healthcare Service Users (Occasional Paper No. 2)*, (Dublin: Schizophrenia Ireland, 2005)

Swanwick GRH, Clare AW, *Suicide in Ireland 1945–1992: Social Correlates*, Irish Medical Journal (90)3, 106–108

WEBSITES

American Association of Suicidology website: www.suicidology.org

Central Statistics Office website: www.cso.ie

IAS website: www.ias.ie

Independent Newspapers Limited: www.unison.ie

International Association for Suicide Prevention Website: www.Iasp.Info

Irish Medical Journal website, http://imj.ie/

Irish Medical Times website, http://www.imt.ie/

The Irish Times: www.ireland.com

Schizophrenia Ireland Website: www.sirl.ie

World Health Organisation Website: www.who.int